REMINISCENCES OF
GOV. R. J. WALKER

GOV. ROBERT J. WALKER.

REMINISCENCES OF GOV. R. J. WALKER

by

GEORGE W. BROWN

The Black Heritage Library Collection

BOOKS FOR LIBRARIES PRESS
FREEPORT, NEW YORK
1972

First Published 1902
Reprinted 1972

F685
B873

INTERNATIONAL STANDARD BOOK NUMBER:
0-8369-8978-3

LIBRARY OF CONGRESS CATALOG CARD NUMBER:
79-38010

PRINTED IN THE UNITED STATES OF AMERICA
BY
NEW WORLD BOOK MANUFACTURING CO., INC.
HALLANDALE, FLORIDA 33009

REMINISCENCES

OF

GOV. R. J. WALKER;

WITH THE TRUE STORY OF

THE RESCUE OF KANSAS FROM SLAVERY.

BY GEO. W. BROWN, M. D.,

HONORARY CORRESPONDING SECRETARY OF THE HISTORICAL
SOCIETY OF KANSAS.

ROCKFORD, ILL.:

PRINTED AND PUBLISHED BY THE AUTHOR.

1902.

DEDICATION.

To Mrs. SARA T. D. ROBINSON,

Oakridge, LAWRENCE, KANSAS—

MADAM:—Permit me to dedicate these humble pages, relating to the pioneer history of your great and prosperous State, to your kindly care. You were identified with all the early settlers who came from the free North and located in and around Lawrence, to whom your hospitality was always cordially extended.

You saw a bald prairie, converted by well-directed toil and genius into the homes of an opulent and free people. You witnessed the aggressions of the slave power, shared in all the hardships and dangers which environed us. Your home was often the council chamber of the Free State leaders. That home with all its valuable contents, was fired by pro-slavery hands, and wholly consumed, May 21, 1856, when my own Herald of Freedom office, with all its presses, type, and fixtures, Miller & Elliot's Free State office, the Emigrant Aid Company's Hotel, were destroyed.

Following this terrible outrage on private rights your husband Charles Robinson, G. W. Smith, G. W. Deitzler, Gaius Jenkins and myself were indicted, by direction of a partisan Court, for high treason; our only offence was laboring by peaceful means to make Kansas free. Held as prisoners for nearly four months, guarded much of the time by a regiment of United States troops you shared the captivity with your husband, and wrote while thus environed, the fullest and most authentic history yet published of those border troubles and pioneer days.

You were also familiar with nearly every transpiring event connected with the great contest, to rescue Kansas from slavery, and were frequently advisory to lines of policy.

While all this is true of yourself, your late husband, by his consummate coolness, courage, careful consideration, and practical
good judgment, was recognized as the head of the Free State
party in all its trials, adversities and triumphs. He was made the
first Governor by the suffrages of a free people, on the admission
of the State into the Union, because of his political, social and
moral worth. He wisely directed the policy of the State during
the major part of the War of the Rebellion. In more pacific
times he laid the foundation of the schools of learning for the
Commonwealth, and contributed largely for their support during
their infancy, donating the domain on which the State University stands, providing by will that his large estate on your de-
mise, shall inure to that University for its endowment. Honored and loved by all classes of a free people, therefore, to you,
Mrs. ROBINSON, to the memory of your departed husband, to the
few survivors of that great struggle for freedom, and to the de-
scendents of those who are gone, to the press, the libraries of
your State, and to all in every clime who, by word or deed, aided
in rescuing Kansas from the curse of slavery, this volume is respectfully inscribed.

PREFACE.

THE SUBSTANCE of these pages was written in 1881, and was published in the Rockford, Ill., *Gazette* where it had a large reading. Many prominent actors in the Kansas strife during its pioneer days, were readers of the paper, while two copies were subscribed for, and are now on file in the Kansas Historical Society. To date, now over twenty years, not a single statement herein made, has been called in question so far as the author has information, yet numerous indorsements have been received from those who had personal knowledge of the subjects treated. Some of these letters will be quoted as notes, else in our closing pages, while their originals in due time will be filed for preservation with the Kansas Historical Society. Many other letters from less prominent persons, indorsing this narrative, are also on file.

At the suggestion of some of the actors, a few points have been elaborated, and new ones in the way of notes have been added, which will make the work more valuable to a new generation and to youthful readers.

The information herein contained could not be given the public, with propriety, at the time of its occurrence. For the want of this information, many pages of what was designed for truthful history, have been distorted, while actors in the exciting incidents, have been misrepresented and frequently maligned. Even recent writers have taken their cue from early press correspondents, ignorant of the truth, or the motive of the actors, and continue to falsify and mislead their readers, giving credit for results to those whose belligerent policy retarded, and sometimes threatened to defeat the grand result of making Kansas a free State.

Having been a personal actor throughout that exciting period in history, the editor and publisher of the HERALD of FREEDOM, the first and leading free state paper in the territory from the beginning to the end of the contest, with intimate relations with all its men of prominence, and as our Kansas success was the real incentive of the South to Secession, ultimating in the extinction of American Slavery, and by reflex action in the principal kingdoms of the world, so while others have placed themselves on record, it seems just that I, too, shall be heard in explanation of many events wherein myself, and those acting with me have been misunderstood and bitterly censured.

I greatly regret I was unable to give a wider circulation to the truth, before so many of the real heroes in the strife had passed away.

"Hear all sides before deciding," is the substance of a Latin proverb with an English rendering. Mine is the "other side" not heretofore so fully told. So much as is contained in this little volume may induce the re-writing of some pages of tangled Kansas history to make them better agree with truth. The whole is submitted in all kindness to the honest and thoughtful consideration of a new generation, in whose hands is the correction of the false in history.   THE AUTHOR.

907 Kilburn Avenue,
        Rockford, Ill.

CHAPTER I.

Introduction.

IN THE autumn of 1879, the author of these pages was solicited to write his recollections of Old John Brown, and Gen. Jas. H. Lane. For reasons sufficient to himself he has chosen to defer writing of Gen. Lane until a future time. While his sketches of Capt. Brown were running through the *Rockford Ill., Gazette*, and several Kansas papers, the reading pnblic were so much interested in them the author was respectfully solicited, by prominent actors in those times, to extend the series so as to embrace most of the leading incidents in the early history of Kansas.

The reader is well aware that the strife between freedom and slavery, beginning with the application for admission of Missouri into the Union in 1820, had increased in intensity until the final repeal of the Missouri Compromise in 1854, and the passage of the Kansas-Nebraska bill, by which those Territories were organized and opened to settlement.

A wild rush of settlers from the North and South to these new regions followed. Each party was determined the institutions of his own section should prevail, to the entire exclusion of the other. Missouri, bounding the Territory on the East, felt that Kansas was positively her own. Her loose population, in advance of the extinguishment of Indian titles, settled along the water courses, and upon the timber lands, selecting valuable claims for neighbors who were expected to follow.

Settlers from the North and East were met at the threshold of the territory, and informed that they should settle in Nebraska; that Kansas was slave Territory; and that at any sacrifice of blood and treasure the South had resolved to make it a slave State. But the brave and adventurous from the North, taking the institutions of their own section with them—a free press, schools and educated labor—marched on, plotted cities, and laid foundations for a great and prosperous Republic.

On the 30th of March, 1855, in response to the proclamation of Governor Reeder ordering an election for members of the General Assembly, armed bodies of men, numbering several thousands in the aggregate, swarmed through the Territory from Missouri, took possession of the polling places, intimidated and drove away the regularly appointed judges, substituted their own men in their places, and elected their own supple tools—generally residents of Missouri—as members of the Legislature. The law-making power thus imposed on the actual residents, a very large majority of whom were in favor of freedom—extended the laws of Missouri over that young empire, and passed others, in what they considered the interests of slavery, which were more bloody in their leading characteristics, than were those accredited to Nero.

The anti-slavery agitation, so long pending in the States and in Congress, was transferred with all its bitterness, to the plains of Kansas. The Northern mind was determined that slavery should not entrench itself on free soil. The South was fully conscious that its favorite institutions could not survive if surrounded by a cordon of free States.

The attempt was first made by *bluster* to prevent Northern people from settling in the Territory. In the autumn of 1853, a public meeting was held at Weston, Mo., presided over by U. S. Senator David Atchison, at which the following was adopted:

"*Resolved,* That if the Territory shall be opened to settlement, we pledge ourselves to each other *to extend the institutions of Missouri over the Territory, at whatever sacrifice of blood and treasure.*"

On June 10th, 1854, ten days only after the bill organizing the territory was signed by the President, a meeting was held at Parkville, Mo., at which, with many others, the following were passed:

"*Resolved,* That we recognize the institution of slavery as already existing in the Territory, and recommend slaveholders to introduce their property as fast as possible.

"*Resolved,* That we afford protection to no Abolitionist as a settler in Kansas Territory."

Similar resolutions were adopted all along the Kansas border, and were published at length in the Missouri papers. They were principally designed to intimidate Northern settlers and prevent them from locating in the contested Territory.

Having control of the legislative power, with the officers and all the machinery of government at their command, they next attempted to enforce the laws they had made.

The discord and violence which followed through the years of 1855, 1856, and which were arrested by

Gov. Geary, in September of the last year; in 1857, under the administration of Gov. Walker, assumed a new form.

The Southern States, observing their waning power, and fully satisfied that they had overdone the *bluster* and *violence* business, changed their policy, and thought by finesse and pacific means, with federal aid, to fasten on the people a pro-slavery Constitution. Gov. Walker, with a national reputation, was sent to Kansas from Mississippi, endorsed by the President and the entire South, with the arms and treasure of the country at his bidding, instructed to secure a faithful expression of the popular will, and the establishment of a government in harmony therewith, but, as the sequel shows, with the purpose of the presidential advisers, to make it a slave State.

This period was the turning point in Kansas history. From it came a free State; the election of President Lincoln; the long and bloody war of Secession; the triumph of federal arms; and the outgrowth is the glorious present and the brilliant future which is just dawning on the American Republic.

Whatever can throw light upon this forming stage in our country's history; this metamorphosis from a divided people—partly slave and partly free—to one of equal rights to all before the law, must necessarily be full of interest to the general reader, and especially to the student. History is but the aggregation of events, succinctly stated. General history is made up of the doings of a large number of people, each of whom has contributed somewhat towards producing the general result. A correct history of any country or event, can not be written until the leading actors have made detailed reports of incidents in which they were individually engaged. So far as they fail to make such reports so far will the general historian be deprived of the requisite material from which to collate a correct history of the times.

Conscious that thousands of others have recollections of thrilling incidents during the eventful times of which I write, yet each one's experience was peculiarly his own, and each contributed his full share towards bringing about the favorable result. Without attempting to rob any one of his just meed of popular applause, to detract one particle from the honors which a grateful posterity will bestow on the *real* heroes in the Kansas struggle, I do propose, in these pages, to write *my own* reminiscences of Gov. Robert J. Walker, with an outline history of the Lecompton Constitution, and the final rescue of Kansas from Slavery. Lovers of fair and impartial history will find much to challenge their attention in these pages, and it is to be hoped those who follow us to the conclusion will be interested and instructed.

CHAPTER II.

Outlines of History.

THE MOST interesting period in Kansas history, and the most important in its consequences to the American Republic is covered by the interval lying between the resignation of Gov. Geary, on the 10th of March, 1857, and the final defeat of the Lecompton Constitution, by a direct vote of the people against it, on the 2d of August, 1858, under the provisions of the so-called English law.

As briefly referred to in our introduction, the pro-slavery residents of Missouri had invaded the Territory, at its first election for delegates to Congress, on the 29th of November, 1854; usurped the franchises of the settlers, and elected J. W. Whitfield to represent them in Congress. They came again by thousands, thoroughly organized, officered and armed, on the 30th of March, 1855; took forcible possession of every polling precinct in the Territory, save one, regardless of the protests of the actual settlers; elected their own men to represent them in the Territorial Legislature, and to frame a code of laws for the government of the people. Gov. Reeder, under duress, issued certificates of election to a majority of the fraudulently elected members. The Legislature was convened under the Governor's direction, at Pawnee, near Fort Riley, on the 2d of July, 1855. A code of laws, highly obnoxious in their pro-

visions upon the slavery question, as upon all other subjects, was passed—the judiciary, *in advance of their
enactment*, declaring them legal.

The people, the actual residents of Kansas, in public conventions, through the press, and on the rostrum, repudiated these "bogus" laws. Collisions followed. Gov. Reeder applied the title of "Border Ruffians * to the invaders, denied the legality of the statutes, and refused to enforce them. He was removed
by President Pierce, and Gov. Shannon succeeded
him.

For a time Gov. Shannon seemed the willing instrument of the slavery propaganda; but before the close
of his administration he discovered his error; at-

* Gov. Reeder soon after the 30th of March visited Washington, hoping to induce Prest. Pierce to disregard the election. On
his way there he stopped at his old home, at Easton, Pa., and told
the story of Kansas' wrongs, in a speech to his old neighbors. In
this he designated the invaders as "Border Ruffians," and said
they were led by their chiefs, David R. Atchison and B. F.
Stringfellow. Soon after the Governor's return to Kansas, he
was called upon by Stringfellow, and a party of kindred spirits.
Stringfellow demanded of Reeder to know if he made the statement. The Governor repeated what he said; that the Territory
had been invaded by a regularly organized company of armed men,
"Border Ruffians," if you please, who took possession of the ballot boxes, and made a Legislature to suit the purposes of the pro-
slavery party; and that in his opinion Gen. Stringfellow was
responsible for the result. Stringfellow sprang to his feet, seized
his chair, and felled the Governor to the floor, kicking him when
down. He also attempted to draw a revolver, but was prevented
from using it by District Attorney Isacks, and Mr. Halderman,
the Governor's private secretary. And this the origin of the
term, so common on the Kansas border for so many years, of
"Border Ruffian." Who shall say it was not well merited. (See
H. of F. Aug, 8, '57, 2d. col., 1st p.)

tempted to correct himself; incurred the displeasure of the ruffian leaders; and was removed by their head at Washington.

Gov. Geary came to Kansas as the successor of Gov. Shannon, in September, 1856. Secretary Woodson, acting Governor, had ordered out the Territorial militia, ostensibly to enforce the bogus laws. Missouri responded, and sent forward a formidable army, bordering closely on three thousand, to crush out the "Free State Insurgents." The latter were in arms for defense. Thus the questions involved were on the eve of a bloody issue when Gov. Geary arrived in the Territory, and interposed the federal army between the belligerents.

A Presidential election was pending in the States. The people of the North were greatly incensed at the action of the federal government, in recognizing and sustaining the usurpers in Kansas. The Republican party was formed out of the Free Soil party, first organized at Buffalo, in 1848, fragments of the disbanded Whig party, with many disaffected and independent members of the Democratic party who were opposed to the aggressions of slavery. Gen. Fremont, the Republican nominee, and the friend of free Kansas, was defeated, and Jas. Buchanan was elected.

A majority of the lower House of Congress were in sympathy with the people of the Territory. They passed laws for the relief of the settlers, but they were invariably defeated in the Senate.

As President Pierce's administration neared its close he attempted more pacific measures for Kansas. His principal adviser, however, was that arch-conspirator, Jefferson Davis, the Secretary of War, and but little was accomplished.

The bogus Legislature of 1855, deferred another session until January, 1857. The second session was held at Lecompton, at which an act was passed making provisions for a Convention to frame a state Constitution. Gov. Geary, on the 18th of February, vetoed the bill, making as his principal objection to it that there was no requirement for submitting the Constitution when framed to the people for their ratification or rejection. The bill was passed over his veto. Provisions were made at the same time for taking a census, for the registry of voters, and the election of sixty delegates, who were to assemble at Lecompton on the third Monday of September following, to commence their labors.

A Free State Convention was held at Topeka on the 10th of March. That body set forth in a preamble that the so-called Legislative Assembly, ordering a Constitutional Convention, was a creature of fraud; that its members were representatives of a people foreign to the Territory; that the organic law did not authorize the Legislature to pass an enabling act, to change the form of government; that the Assembly was partisan in its character; that it clearly contemtemplated further fraud and violence; that it deprives the Executive of power to prevent or remedy such fraud; that it leaves the control of the census, the registry of voters, the apportionment of members, and the whole machinery pertaining to the election in the hands of pretended officers not elected by the people; and that there is no provision for submitting the Constitution so framed to the voters for their approval or otherwise. The Convention then resolved that they could not participate in such election without compromising their rights as American citizens, sacrificing the best interests of Kansas, and jeopardizing the public peace.

On the same day with the assembling of this Convention at Topeka, Gov. Geary, fearful of assassination from the more violent of the pro-slavery party—which had been several times attempted—sent his resignation to the President, and quietly left the Territory, issuing a farewell address to the people, dated on the 12th, filled with valuable advice and suggestions for preserving the public tranquility.

On the 10th of April following, ROBERT J. WALKER, of Mississippi, was commissioned Governor, and FRED. P. STANTON, of Tennessee, was appointed Secretary.

Daniel Woodson, of Virginia, was the first Secretary of Kansas, serving from June 29th, 1854, through the whole period of Governor Reeder's, Shannon's and Geary's administrations, officiating as Acting Governor during the absence of these functionaries from the Territory, and during vacations. He was a willing tool of the slave power; and, during the periods he was acting Governor, the Kansas troubles were at their greatest hight.

Secretary Stanton visited Lawrence for the first on the 24th of April, 1857, one month in advance of the arrival of Gov. Walker, and was Acting Governor during the interim. He was received by the people of the city with great cordiality, was entertained by Gov. Robinson at dinner, and at the Cincinnati

House in the evening, where he partook of a supper with many leading citizens. During the evening, he was called on by the people generally, for a speech. In the course of his remarks he said:

"You wish to know my position in regard to the Territorial laws. Congress has recognized them as binding. A majority of that body gave Whitfield a seat as a Territorial delegate, and made appropriations for carrying on the Government. President Buchanan has recognized the laws as valid, and they must be received as such. [Never! from the multitude.] You must obey them, and pay the taxes. [*Never!* no NEVER!] There is where I am at war with you. [Then let there be war.] It shall be war to the knife, and knife to the hilt! I say it without excitement, and wish you to receive it as such; the taxes must be collected, and it becomes the duty of my administration to see that they are collected. [Then you bring the government into collision with them.]

Aside from this episode, the speech of Acting Governor Stanton was well received. But here seemed the elements of future discord, which Gov. Geary's six months' pacific administration just closed, had almost wholly allayed.

I introduce this incident to show the condition of the public pulse, and the determination of the officials at the time of Gov. Walker's arrival at Lawrence, just five weeks thereafter.

CHAPTER III.

Arrival of Governer Walker.

GOV. WALKER reached Leavenworth on the 25th, and Lawrence on the 26th of May, 1857. He had been accompanied up the Missouri by Senator Wilson, of Massachusetts. Rev. John Pierpont, and Dr. Howe reached Lawrence a day in advance of the Governor, and arrangements had been made for a temperance meeting, at the Unitarian Church, on Tuesday evening. Gov. Walker, who tarried over night in Lawrence, was in attendance.

I am sure my Kansas readers will allow a slight digression, while I recite brief paragraphs in the remarks of Senator Wilson and Rev. Pierpont, complimentary of the country, made on that occasion. Said Mr. Wilson:

"I have never seen a more pleasantly located place than Lawrence, or a more fertile region than that surrounding the city. I do not think there is another such a lovely site for a town on the western continent. [Turning to Mr. Pierpont,] Perhaps my venerable friend, who has traveled all over the old world, may have seen a more beautiful landscape, or more enchanting scenery. [Mr. P. answered "No, sir!"] He says 'No, sir.' I did not know but he might somewhere, in his many wanderings, have found a lovelier spot, but I have not seen it."

Rev. Pierpont, possibly inspired by Mr. Wilson's appeal to him, in the course of his address, which followed, said:

"I have probably traveled more than most men of my profession, having journeyed all over the United States, and visited each of them, save those on the Pacific coast; I have wandered through the East, looked out upon the gorgeous scenery of Northern and Middle Europe, on the vine-clad vales of the Rhine, and down from the Alpine heights of Switzerland; I have traveled through sunny Italy, classic Greece, the land of Pyramids, Holy Palestine, but in all my wanderings I have never looked upon a more beautiful prospect than that which I beheld from Mt. Oread to-day. I can well say, in the amended language of another, 'God might have made a more lovely country, but I am sure He has never done it.'"

Gov. Walker spoke briefly, but he touched upon those subjects in which all were interested. He referred to his inaugural, which would be published the next day, embracing his views in detail. Among other things he said:

"I recognize no right but that of the majorty, to decide the sectional questions which have disturbed the Territory. Upon that basis I shall rest the administration of Kansas affairs; and it will be my endeavor to establish that principle, and make it so complete that the difficulties now existing may be obviated in the shortest way. The people—the actual *bona fide* settlers, and none others, shall be allowed the right of suffrage. This is guaranteed to you, and it shall be my province, while I remain your Governor, to enforce to the fullest extent, your legal rights in this regard."

The masses of the people were very much pleased with Gov. Walker's avowals, and leading men did not hesitate to so express themselves to him.

On Wednesday, the 27th of May, he continued his journey to Lecompton, where he read his inaugural, which, it was afterwards stated, was prepared in

Washington, and submitted to President Buchanan, who approved of it, also to a few friends in New York, as well as to Senator Douglas, whom the Governor called upon in Chicago. In his address he declared himself devoted to the Union, believing that upon its preservation depended the hopes, not of this country alone, but of the world. He was profoundly anxious to remove everything which endangered its peace, or menaced its existence. The Kansas question, in his judgment, constituted the most serious of the perils with which it is now environed; and he hoped if this could be fairly and satisfactorily adjusted the last of the dangers which threatened its peace and prosperity would be dispelled.

While tarrying in New York, on his way to Kansas, a few personal friends gave him a public entertainment. In response to a toast on that occasion he said:

"Nothing could have induced me to accept the office of Governor of Kansas, tendered me by the President, but the hope of restoring peace to that Territory, and of doing something to settle decisively and finally the great controversy which has divided the country and which is the only thing endangering the peace and stability of the Union."

Gov. Walker's name was familiar to the entire country. A native of Pennsylvania, and a son of one of the distinguished Judges of the Supreme Court of that commonwealth; a lawyer by education; locating in Mississippi in early manhood, he became identified with the material interests of the state. He filled various responsible positions in the local government; was elected to the United States Senate, which impor-

tant position he filled from 1837 to 1845; then, as
Secretary of the Treasury, he was a leading member
in President Polk's cabinet.   In 1846, he revised the
tariff system of the country, and his project became a
law almost as it came from his hands.   To his great
credit it can be said, one of his official reports on the
finances of the country, was published at length, at
the instance of Sir Robert Peel, in the London *Times,*
the only document of that character which ever
receied such marked consideration in a foreign country.   Gov. W. married a grand-daughter of Benjamin
Franklin.*

In coming to Kansas, he was welcomed with great
cordiality by all classes.   The pro-slavery men saw in
him a member of their own party, sympathizing fully
with Southern institutions, and ready at all times, as
they hoped, to advance their interests at whatever
sacrifice.   Many of the Free State men, indeed, perhaps all at first, were apprehensive that, with his
superior executive ability, great talent and personal
popularity in the South, he would so manage affairs
as to fasten slavery upon the people as a permanent
institution.   Correspondents of the Eastern press
located in Kansas, commenced denouncing him before
his arrival, and they continued that course long after
he left the Territory.   Not content with assailing
him, they were violent in their abuse of all Free State
men who were on friendly terms with him, and who

*Gov. Robert J. Walker was born in Northumberland, Pa.,
July, 23. 1801.   He died in Washington, D. C., Nov. 11, 1869.
He was educated at the University of Pennsylvania, studied law
with his father, married a daughter of Franklin Bache, a grand-
daughter of Benjamin Franklin.

said, wrote or published a kindly word in his defense. Even a small portion of the Kansas press pursued a similar line of policy, and, so far as it had the power, embittered many good men against him at the outset.

The writer had the pleasure of listening to the Governor's few remarks at the Unitarian Church, and reported portions of them which were published in the *Herald of Freedom* of May 30. He thought he saw in him a desire to deal justly by all, and determined that he would do nothing, with word or pen, to drive him to antagonism with the Free State party.

CHAPTER IV.

Interview with Gov. Walker.

On Saturday, the 30th of May, Gov. Walker returned to Lawrence, from Lecompton, and again stopped at the Morrow House. He was waited upon by many of our leading citizens, who welcomed him and his escort to the Territory.

On Sunday morning, Sec'y Stanton and E. O. Perrine, who came to Kansas with the Secretary, and who became famed among the people for his brilliant speeches, and who was popularly known as "Spread-Eagle Perrine," called upon the writer, at the sanctum of the HERALD OF FREEDOM office, and stated that among the many callers on the Governor the day before the neglect of the editor to visit him had been noted; that the Governor had remarked about it, and, as his stay in Lawrence would be brief, it would give him pleasure to have an interview.

"Please say to the Governor," I replied, "that he has mistaken our positions. I am the editor of the *Herald of Freedom*, Mr. Walker is a mere Territorial Governor, an office so humble, judging by the number who have filled that station during the last year or two, as hardly to be worthy of mention. Tell the Governor I shall be sincerely glad to see him, and shall welcome him with great cordiality to my *sanctum sanctorum*, but I cannot think for a moment of leaving my tripod to visit merely a Kansas Governor."

"You mean, simply that as the mountain will not go to Mohamet, Mohamet must go to the mountain," replied Stanton, laughing.

"That is it exactly."

"A good joke," said Perrine. "I will report you, word for word to the Governor; and unless I mistake his make-up you may expect a call from him this morning."

I begged him to modulate the remarks somewhat, if I was to he reported; but be assured us it would be reported *verbatim*. Placing himself in. position he repeated the speech, whilst Stanton seemed ready to burst with laughter.

They left, begging me not to leave the office for a short time.

Perhaps twenty minutes elapsed, when the same gentlemen returned with Gov. Walker, and we were introduced. Yet holding the Governor's hand, and standing near the door, I said:

"Governor, I understand you are a native of Pennsylvania."

"I was born there, sir, and spent the early years of my life in that State, and I still look upon the old Keystone as the brightest in the federal arch."

"I hail from that State, and indorse your sentiment," said I.

"Indeed, from what county?"

"Crawford."

"From Crawford county! Why, Mr. Brown, I spent the first years of my life after my graduation in that county, surveying for the Holland Land Company."

"You know Mr. Huidekoper, then?"

"I was in the employ of Harm Jan Huidekoper, and when I left his service he presented me with a purse, [I think he said three thousand dollars], with which I purchased my law library—locating in Pittsburg."

"Why, my father purchased his lands," said I, "of Mr. Huidekoper," telling him where they were located.

"I remember that region well. John B. Wallace owned lands in that section. How strange. Those old names come back to me so strongly. Alexander Power, a surveyor, must have been near you."

"Yes, I understand he took a quantity of land in part payment for his services. Conneautville is located on his lands."

"Why, Mr. Brown, we are old acquaintances. I am really glad to meet you."

All this time we had remained standing. Taking chairs we talked of others of the old settlers about Meadville, most of whom I had known in my boyhood; all of whom had since passed away.

The Governor then remarked that he had been having a very rich experience for the last few weeks. "Four weeks ago to-day," said he, "I was in New York. I thought I would like to hear that eccentric preacher, Henry Ward Beecher. So I paid a visit to his church. He gave us a genuine anti-slavery speech. If he had known I was in the audience I should have believed it was designed expressly for my ears; but it was impossible for him to have known I was there. The following Sunday I spent

Buffalo. There I had the pleasure of listening to another anti-slavery sermon. I came up the Missouri on a steamer with Senator Wilson. The passengers teased him to make a speech, and of course it was anti-slavery. To-day I am going to the Unitarian church to hear Rev. Mr. Nute. I expect I shall be entertained with another sermon of the same sort. Possibly they will convert me to their views yet," with a hearty laugh, in which all joined. Looking at his watch, and turning to Mr. Stanton, he continued, "I see it is time we were on our way to church. Mr. Brown, I want a long interview with you. At what hour can I see you?"

"Consult your own convenience, Governor. I can be at leisure at any time."

"Two o'clock, then, promptly at two o'clock I shall call upon you. I must not miss that anti-slavery sermon."

I am thus particular in repeating this my first interview with Gov. Walker, at length, as furnishing *in part* a key to the pleasant relations which afterwards existed between us, and which, I am glad to write, were in no manner interrupted for a single moment. As we proceed with these 'Reminiscences' I trust the reader will see the importance attached to this and the afternoon interview in moulding the future of Kansas, of the National government, and, may I not add, of the world?

CHAPTER V.

FIFTEEN minutes before two o'clock Gov. Walker called again at the HERALD OF FREE-DOM office. He made no mention whatever of the church service. He was unattended and appeared in excellent spirits. Being seated, he began:

"Mr. Brown, I had a long interview with Gov. Geary before leaving Washington in regard to Kansas matters. He told me of you, and requested me to make your acquaintance. He represented you as an honest, conscientious and truthful journalist, strongly anti-slavery, but opposed to all sorts of disorder and violence. He said any statement you may make to me I can rely upon implicitly. Now I would like to have you give me a full and detailed account of your troubles, their causes, and any suggestions you may be pleased to make for their avoidance in the future. I wish you to give me especially your views of Governors Reeder and Shannon, and I do not wish you to make any reservation because of our party diffier-ences. I am an inquirer after truth, and I have come to Kansas with an earnest determination to right your wrongs so far as I have the ability." He then went on to say that the strife in Kansas was only a removal to another field of a long struggle in the South, headed by Calhoun, looking to a dissolution of the Union. He had met and fought it on every stump in

Mississippi. "Why, Mr. Brown, I literally wrapped the flag of my country around my person, in some of my campaign speeches in the South, and declared that when I died I would die under its protecting folds. I meant, it sir, not as a rhetorical flourish, but as a simple fact.* You of the North have another set of extremists, with the same ends in view, urging a different cause for reaching that end; but they are revolutionists and disunionists nevertheless, and it is the duty of all good men everywhere to unite, put an end to these difficulties, and the dangers threatening us. Unless we do so but a few years will find us engaged in a fratricidal war, the most calamitous in its results of any which has ever visited the world. I hope to do my share in Kansas to avert those consequences. Now begin, commencing with Gov. Reeder's administration."

I then gave the Governor a short sketch of the leading events connected with Gov. Reeder's administration. Mentioned the first election of a Delegate to Congress, on the 29th of November, 1854, and of the scenes of violence and disorder enacted at Leavenworth, as furnished me by my own special correspondent, who was on the ground. Passing this, I gave him an account of the invasion of every election

*Perhaps it is as well in this place as any other to state that on the breaking out of the war of the Rebellion, Gov. Walker became an intimate acquaintance of President Lincoln, and because of his great financial reputation, was sent to Europe, where he negotiated sales for $250,000,000 of United States bonds, giving great relief to our pecuniary necessities for ready money to prosecute the war. He published four pamphlets in England on the finances and resources of the United States, in 1863--4.

precinct save one, on the 30th of March, 1855, by an
armed body of strangers from Missouri, who came in
force, nominated and elected their own men to seats
in the Legislative Assembly, excluding the Free State
settlers from the polls, or allowing a few to vote
near the close of the day; that they took the election
returns with them to the Shawnee Mission, near the
Missouri border, where Gov. Reeder was sojourning,
and compelled him, under threats of violence, to issue
certificates of election to a majority of the members
of the first Legislature thus fraudulently elected. I
said: "This was Gov. Reeder's first great error."

"Consented to do, and did a great wrong, from fear
of personal violence. Why, Mr. Brown, I would have
suffered the amputation of my right hand before I
would have done such an act; yes, would been bored
throught by a bullet. You do justly in holding Gov.
Reeder responsible for the consummation of that terrible wrong which bad men had inaugurated. But
I am interrupting you. Proceed."

I then gave an account of the second election which
Gov. Reeder had ordered, to elect new members in
those districts to which he had not issued certificates
of election.

"A silly act," replied the Governor. "All parliamentary bodies decide upon the rights of its own
members to seats. A majority of that Legislature
held certificates of election from the Governor. They
constituted a quorum for business, and as such, could
give the residue of the seats to whom they pleased."

I stated that the body so acted when convened at
Pawnee, on the 2d day of July following, and that

all holding certificates from the Governor, issued for the second election, were removed, and the invaders from Missouri were given the seats in their stead. I then gave the Governor a specimen of "hasty legislation," which I witnessed at Pawnee on the 4th of July, 1855. Dr. J. H. Stringfellow introduced a bill in the lower House, on the morning of that day, with the statement:

"I hold in my hand a bill, more important in its consequences, than that signed by the fathers of the American revolution, seventy-nine years ago to-day. The Declaration of Independence gave freedom to America. This bill which I shall introduce will perpetuate it. I ask immediate action on the subject, and hope the House will suspend the rules, and allow it to pass through all the parliamentary stages, without the usual delay."

· He read substantially as follows:

"Be it Enacted by the Governor and Legislative Assembly of the Territory of Kansas: That the general laws of Missouri, not locally inapplicable, be and the same are hereby enacted and extended over the Territory of Kansas,"

Some member, I think it was Mr. Wilkinson, of Pottawatomie Creek, moved to amend by substituting the statutes of Tennessee. He said he was acquainted with the laws of that State, but not of Missouri, therefore he preferred the amendment. Another member sprang to his feet and said:

"Both, the statutes of Missouri and Tennessee protect the institution of slavery, and that is enough for me to know. I am prepared to vote for the bill as it now stands."

The motion to amend was not seconded. The rules were suspended, and in one hour from the introduc-

tion of the bill it had passed its several readings, and,
as far as the Lower House was concerned, it possessed
all the elements of a law. It was signed by the
Speaker, and carried by a messenger to the Council.
I followed the messenger to that body, and saw the
bill introduced; but my recollection is, it was referred
to a committee, and delayed in its final passage until
the body had removed, a few days after, to the Shawnee Mission. [It is proper to state that the House
Journal does not make mention of this proceeding.
Mr. Wattles, in his history of Kansas, published in
the *Herald of Freedom*, applies this language of
Stringfellow's to another measure, and says that "An
act to establish the statutes of the Territory of Kansas," was introduced on the 5th. I made notes of the
transaction at the time, and feel confident that I am
not mistaken in this statement.]

The Governor laughed heartily over the incident
as I narrated it, and said: "There are fanatics in all
legislative bodies, and it is evident Stringfellow is
troubled in that direction."

I then called his attention to the laws they passed,
among others making it a criminal offense, punish-
able in the penitentiary, to write, print, publish or
declare that slavery has not a legal existence in
Kansas."

"Were not those unwise laws repealed at the late
session of the Legislative Assembly?"

"Some of them were, but enough are left to damn
any law-making body."

"Did Gov. Reeder sign those laws?"

"No, he repudiated the action of the Legislature

after its removal to the Mission, and he was soon after removed by the president."

"Well what of Gov. Shannon?"*

"Our whole people gave him the cold shoulder on his arrival in the Territory. He was welcomed, and feasted, and wined by pro-slavery leaders, and looked upon the actual settlers as outlaws, and, for a time, treated them as such. He brought on the Wakarusa war, by calling the Territorial militia into service against the Free State settlers. His militia consisted almost wholly of the rowdy and drinking element in Missouri, who responded to his call, and came over in organized companies, with all the munitions of war, swearing vengeance against the 'd—d Yankee paupers at Lawrence.'"

"There was no collision between your people and the Governor's forces?"

"No. As soon as the facts were made known to the Governor, he disbanded his 'militia' and sent them back into Missouri."

"The sacking of Lawrence, the destruction of the

*Gov. Wilson Shannon was a lawyer of some prominence. In 1838 he was elected Governor of Ohio; was defeated by Tom Corwin in 1840, re-elected in 1842; in 1844 was made Minister to Mexico; in 1853 was elected to Congress; in 1855 was appointed by President Pierce as Governor of Kansas. Resigned in the summer of 1856; subsequently located with his family in Law-, rence, where he was in the practice of law until his death, August 30, 1897. Gov. Shannon was a man of sterling integrity, of first class legal ability, and only lacked efficient firmness to resist, at the outset, the demands of the pro-slavery leaders in Kansas. He died universally respected by all parties. His wife, whom he married in Harrison County, Ohio, survived him, and died in January, 1881, universally beloved.

Free State presses, your *Herald of Freedom* office included, and the demolition of the hotel as a nuisance, was under his administration?"

"Yes;" and I gave him a brief history of the outrages.

"Sent here to protect the people, and conniving at their destruction. I have no sympathy with such transactions. Gov. Shannon left the Territory under a cloud, did he not?"

"Yes, after the destruction of Lawrence he seemed to fall into bad odor with the leaders of his party. He had been applied to for United States troops to aid in assessing and collecting taxes under the bogus laws. He refused to lend the army for such services. It is said for this reason his associate officers and party generally opposed him, and succeeded in securing his removal. They threatened him with a bath in the river before leaving. It was reported that he went in some sort of disguise, in a government conveyance, to Fort Leavenworth, where he took a steamer down the Missouri."

"I think Gov. Geary told me you, with others, were indicted for high treason. What was your offense?"

"For publishing a Free State newspaper, I suppose. We were charged with levying war against the Government; but this was only *constructively*. Judge Lecompton instructed the Grand Jurors that advising resistance to the Territorial laws was *constructive high treason*, and if the jurors found any persons had so advised, to find indictments against them."

"Under our Constitution we have no constructive high treason. An *overt act* must be committed to constitute the crime, and this must be proved by two witnesses. You had no trial?"

"No; we were held some four months as prisoners, refused bail, guarded a portion of the time by a regiment of United States troops, then released on our personal recognizances to the next term of court, when the indictment was *nolle prossed.*"

"The Legislature last winter passed a law calling a convention to frame a State Constitution, I am told. What are your people going to do about it?"

"Nothing."

"Is that wise?"

"We think so."

"Why do you take such a position? It seems to me you are imperiling everything. You claim that your friends are largely in the majority. If so, it occurs to me, that it is your duty to engage in the election, send up a majority who favor your views, and form a constitution in harmony with them. In this way you can easily slide out of your Territorial condition into that of a State, and get rid of all your political troubles."

"I apprehend, Governor, that you take a wrong view of this question. The Legislature provided for the taking of the census, and the registry of the voters of the Territory, and made a provision that no person should be allowed to vote for delegates to the convention whose name is not registered. There is no power in the people to correct that register. The work has been done, so far as done at all, by violent pro-slavery men, and they have been careful to exclude nearly all the Free State men from the register. It is impos-

sible under the law, with the fraudulent registration,
to elect a Free State delegation from any district in
the Territory. No provision is made for submitting
the constitution to the people. It is wholly a one-
sided affair, and, as such, we have decided to pay no
attention to it, and resist its adoption by Congress."

"A very unsafe proceeding. The President and
Senate are understood to favor the formation of a
State Constitution, as the easiest way of getting rid of
you. You cannot count with safety on the House.
But we will waive that matter. You are to have a
new election the coming autumn for a Delegate to
Congress, and for a Legislative Assembly. What
action will your people take on these matters?"

"They have resolved not to participate in any
election held under the bogus laws; and as the ballot-
box is hedged in, no Free State man can participate
in the election under them without dishonor."

"To what do you refer?"

"A test oath is required of all who vote, that they
will sustain those villainous laws, and they are required
to pay a poll tax of one dollar."

"Suppose I issue a proclamation declaring any
such provisions inoperative and void; that the elections must be held under the provisions of the organic
act, without regard to your local legislation? How,
then, will your people feel in regard to voting?"

"If we could have satisfactory assurance that we
shall have a fair and impartial election; that none but
bona fide residents of the Territory shall participate
in the elections; that fraudulent returns shall be dis-
regarded, by the election committee of which your
honor and the Secretary are members, and a major-

ity; and the objectional features just mentioned shall be ignored, I think the Free State party will engage in the election. I feel like doing so, and will use the *Herald of Freedom* to influence the party in that direction."

Mr. Brown, your propositions seem just, and I now give you my pledge that each suggestion you have made shall be carried out to the letter, on condition you will get your party to participate in the elections."

" I promise you only as regards the election of a delegate to Congress, and for members of the Legislative Assembly."

" Suppose the Constitution is submitted to a full vote of the people, will you not vote for its reception or rejection?"

" Governor, we cannot so far recognize the bogus Legislature, as to vote even against a Constitution framed by its authority. If, however, the instrument, as an entirety, is submitted to the whole people of Kansas, and our friends can have assurances of a fair chance under it, possibly they may be induced to vote it down; but I will not promise at present to favor such a measure through my paper."

" We agree very well. There is another matter I wish to compare views with you—that is, in regard to the collection of taxes. What are your views in regard to them?"

"That we will resist their collection to the extent of our power."

" You do not mean to be understood that you would advise forcible resistance?"

" I mean, Governor, that the people of Kansas occupy the same position in regard to these laws, and taxes imposed under them, as did our revolutionary ancestors in regard to the tax levied by the British government on the colonies. The body imposing these taxes on the people of Kansas was foreign to the soil; it had no interest in common with us; we had no voice in its election, and we cannot consent to be governed by it, or forced to contribute of our means for its support. We have been anxious to make a case for the Supreme Court, where this matter may be fully adjudicated."

"You are aware, Mr. Brown, that the President recognizes these laws, to which you object, as valid; he has instructed me, as your Executive, to so treat them; and has placed the military forces of the United States subject to my order to put down any opposition to their enforcement. I do not wish any collision with your people and will do all I can to avert any; but from your position I cannot see how it can be avoided. Suppose I am called upon, as I probably will be, by the Sheriff to furnish a military force to aid in the collection of taxes. Under my instructions what am I to do but furnish him such force?"

"Do this, Governor, procrastinate action until after the October election. If you give us a fair and impartial election, as you have promised, our people will engage in it. If we elect all the officers, or a majority, even, who are opposed to those laws, or who favor their repeal, then you will not be called upon after such election for the *posse* you contemplate. If we are defeated by fair means, then it will be evident we are in the minority, and we ought to pay the taxes, and I will no longer oppose their collection?"

"I like your position, Mr. Brown, and am inclined

to favor your suggestion. Possibly we could do the same way as to all the statutes, and delay their execution, other than as regards the elections, until the whole matter shall be thus settled in October. I will talk with Secretary Stanton in regard to the matter; but without regard to his views I will agree not to use the troops to aid in the collection of taxes until after the October election, and not then if you Free State men get control of the elective offices."

"Thank you, Governor, for your decision. I shall hold you to this, as to the other promises you have made." I then called his attention to an editorial in the *Herald of Freedom* of April 18th, headed "There is Hope," written soon after his appointment We said:

"From all the information we are able to collect from our exchanges, we are not without hope in regard to our new Governor. It is true he is a Southern man, residing in the extreme South, but he is not an ultraist, nor a disunionist. If he consults the best interests of Kansas, and regards the will of the majority, and does justice by all parties, we are satisfied. We do not ask for the Free State Party any special privileges. *Give us equal and exact justice*, and no man shall ever find a word of censure for him in the *Herald of Freedom*; on the contrary, if he will labor to correct abuses in this Territory, we will exert our humble influence to strengthen his administration, by presenting him properly before the public. Others may oppose us, as they have in the past, and may labor to embarrass Gov. W. in the discharge of his official duties; we shall not, unless we are satisfied his intentions are to oppose us, and enslave the people, then we shall not hesitate to 'let slip the dogs of war.' "

"This is more, Mr. Brown, than I asked, or even expected. I am truly glad I have met you; glad I have made your acquaintance; glad you extended the olive branch to me, before I started Kansas-ward; glad you are from Pennsylvania, my native State, in which I have always taken great pride. I give my hand, as a token of personal friendship. Whatever I can do to advance your interests please command me."

Our interview lasted several hours, and it was in no way interrupted. It made a favorable and lasting impression on my mind as to the good intentions of the Governor, and from that hour I felt the freedom of Kansas was fully assured.

CHAPTER VI.

Gov. Walker's Inaugural.

IN HIS Inaugural Address, of date May 27, 1857, Gov. Walker took occasion to urge the people of Kansas to participate in the election of delegates to the Constitutional Convention. He assured them that "the authority of the Convention is distinctly recognized in my instructions from the President." He said: "I cannot doubt that the Convention, after having formed a State Constitution, will submit it for ratification or rejection to a majority of the then actual *bona fide* resident settlers of Kansas." He stated that his instructions were to sustain the regular Legislature in assembling a Convention to frame a State Constitution; and that in submitting it to the people, "the fair expression of the popular will must not be interrupted by fraud or violence." The Governor labored at great length to convince the people that their interests favored the formation of a State government. In regardt o the slavery question he said:

"There is a law more powerful than the legislation of man, more potent than passion or prejudice, that must ultimately determine the location of slavery in this country. It is the isothermal line, it is the law of the thermometer, of latitude or altitude, regulating climate, labor and productions, and, as a consequence, of profit and loss." He promised a glowing future for Kansas, "a career of power, progress and prosperity unsurpassed in the history of the world," if the questions growing out of slavery were peacefully settled by the people, while, in vivid contrast, he showed the effects if this strife was prolonged. "Fraud, violence and injustice will reign supreme throughout our borders, and we will have achieved the undying infamy of having destroyed the liberty of our country and the world. We will become a byword of reproach and obloquy; and all history will record the fact that 'Kansas was the grave of the American Union.'" He closed his long address, filling a page in the *Herald of Freedom*, of June 6, 1857, with laudations of the American Constitution, and unshaken trust in an overrulingProvidence, saying, "It is this hand which beckons us onward in the pathway of peaceful progress, expansion and renown, until our continent, in the distant future, shall be covered with the folds of the American banner, and, instructed by our example, all the nations of the world, through many trials and sacrifices, shall establish the great principles of our constitutional confederacy of free and sovereign States."

This Inaugural was published in most of the papers in Kansas, was distributed in large numbers in pamphlet form among the people, and was generally very well received. Of the Governor and his address the writer of these pages at the time, in a leading editorial in his paper, said:

"The policy of Gov. Walker is a policy the people of Kansas have reason to hail with delight. It will release them from political thraldom, it will give them possession of all their God-given rights. The Territorial Legislature laid a plan to perpetuate their power, but through the kindly instrumentality of Gov. Walker they will signally fail."

CHAPTER VII.

Strife Brewing.

GOV. WALKER, accompanied by Secretary Stanton and E. O. Perrin, visited Topeka on the 6th of June, and each addressed the people at length. Here the Governor delivered his real inaugural. That of the 27th, as before stated, was prepared in Washington, while yet unacquainted with the people he was going out to govern; the address at Topeka was evidently an extemporaneous effort, with the people of Kansas before him. He was still solicitous they should participate in the election, and made this the burden of his logic. He claimed that since the President and Congress recognized the Territorial authorities, there was no other way by which our lost rights could be regained. The Governor pledged the people anew that they should have justice at the ballot box; that no invasion from Missouri or elsewhere would be allowed to influence or control the election; that the Constitution about to be framed shall be submitted in its entirety, to the whole people, that if it is not so submitted, he will join in opposing it; that they can get control of the Territorial government in October if they have a *bona fide* majority of voters, repeal the obnoxious laws, and enact new ones such as the majority shall approve.

The Governor argued at length against the Topeka Constitution; showed that organization with an attempt to enforce any pretended laws enacted under it would be revolutionary, and that he could not allow any action of that character.

During his speech the Governor was asked: "What of the taxes?" As if recalling his agreement made with the writer on the 30th of May, only eight days before, he replied: "Long before I am called upon for any official action, the reign of law, of justice, and the people will be so fully established here, that, as good citizens, you will cheerfully pay this small pittance to support your own government."

While Gov. Walker was making this pacificatory speech in Topeka, Deputy Marshal Faine, who was also Deputy Sheriff and Assessor, was in the vicinity of Lawrence attempting to levy taxes. This was no doubt expressly designed by the pro-slavery revolutionists as an element of strife, hoping to enlist the Governor in their mad schemes, and force him into collision with the Free State people.

The latter had learned of the intentions of these agitators, and held a public meeting in Lawrence, Col. James Blood in the chair, in which they solemnly resolved they would pay no taxes imposed.

About the same time a movement was on foot in Lawrence to organize an independent city government. This last movement was not generally favored by the property holders. However, springing from those who participated in the election, a charter was made and adopted, and officers were elected under it.

Rumors were continually rife that the "fire-eaters" at Lecompton were daily importuning the Governor for United States troops to send to Lawrence to aid in the assessment and collection of taxes, and to prevent the Topeka Legislature from assembling.

The Topeka Legislature assembled on the 9th of June. They continued in session until the 13th, and adjourned *sine die*, first making provision for its own perpetuation, that it might be used in case of necessity.

On the 15th of June that portion of the "registered" voters of Kansas, who desired, engaged in the election of delegates to a Constitutional Convention, under bogus authority, no Free State men participating in such election. Though Gov. Walker had repeatedly given it as his opinion that the voting population of the Territory equaled 25,000 to 30,000, yet a trifle less than 2,000 votes were polled, and many of these were fraudulent. Whole counties, quite densely populated, had no chance for representation; however the census was not taken in such counties, neither were any voters registered, without which they had no right to vote under the law.

CHAPTER VIII.

A Policy for the Future.

THE LEADING editorial in the *Herald of Freedom* of July 4, 1857, defined at length the writer's position in regard to the future policy of that paper, and what was deemed by the editor, indispensable to the final success of the Free State party. Before putting it in type we invited a dozen or more personal friends, gentlemen who had been frequent contributors to the paper, to meet at our office, to whom we read the article at length, and asked each in turn his candid opinion of the program. Among the number present was our associate, Augustus Wattles; our head clerk, A. P. Nixon; and foreman, H. Bisbee; John M. Coe, Erastus Heath, E. S. Lowman, Judge G. W. Smith, and, if we remember rightly, J. S. Emery and Joel K. Goodin were of that number. Each one fully approved of the editorial, and promised to labor with voice and pen, to carry out in good faith the propositions. Knowing full well the violent opposition the new position would meet from our own party friends, we took this action to know on whom we could rely during the protracted controversy which would inevitably follow. The importance of that editorial justifies its publication entire. It was headed, "The Past—A Plan for the Future." We quote:

"In another place will be found the leading editorial which was published in the first number of the

Herald of Freedom. That number was worked off
on our power press, in Pennsylvania, before taking it
down to ship to Kansas. *Twenty-one thousand copies*
were printed, bearing date October 21st, 1854, though
it was actually printed as early as the 20th of September previous. We re-publish it, that all our present readers may see where we stood at *that* time—
our motive in coming here, as indicated in the fore
part of March of that year—what our hopes were,
and the instrumentalities we desired to employ in
working the freedom of Kansas. Devoted then, as
now, to the American Union; believing that all our
political ills could be cured by the ballot box; and
believing that Kansas was rich in the natural elements which are the foundations of wealth, we relied
upon the press to develop the resources of the country, induce a heavy immigration, and through that
emigration to control the political destinies of the
Territory.

"It was not a part of our programme, *nor never has
been*, to array ourselves against the Federal Union.
As a Republican, we believed in the doctrine that the
majority must rule; if they cannot rule by the ballot, they will be the minority in strength, when the
issue is decided by the sword, and might as well submit first as last.

"Our troubles came on here in Kansas. The majority were beaten and ground down by invaders from
abroad, and the principles of republicanism were
crushed for the time. Notwithstanding this, we have
always been strong in the faith that the majority
would triumph. In the language of our leader,
referred to, 'We might be stricken down at first, but
not defeated.' In the darkest hours of our Territorial history, when the black cloud enveloped the whole
horizon, and our people were driven with violence
from the Territory, and the air was filled with smoke
from burning dwellings, the earth was wet with
human gore, and the dead and dying blocked up the

road—though a prisoner, charged with an infamous crime, and denied all intercourse with the outer world; yet never for a moment did we despond. Through all the clouds and darkness we saw a brighter day, and rejoiced at the prospect of peace, the triumph of the right, and the restoration of order.

"Political sunlight gradually dawned. The clouds did not recede at once; but one by one they sank below the horizon. With an abiding faith in the wisdom of Providence, a firm reliance on His interposition to secure the triumph of justice, we have waited and watched the development of affairs. Though but one year has intervened, how different the aspect of the country to-day from what it was at that period. Now peace and tranquility reign on every hand. Others may prognosticate evil, and tell us it is the quiet which precedes the storm, yet the calm observer knows such is not the case. Our civil rights are now within our reach, and nothing but impolitic action or 'masterly inactivity' can defeat us.

" With a population of twenty for freedom to one against it, we must go to work. We must work unitedly and effectually. We must work to *triumph,* and if we cannot have the selection of implements for working our disenthrallment, we must use those of the enemy. Never, save in Kansas, have we known a people too fastideous to use the arms of an enemy to work their liberation from slavery. The Israelites did not hesitate to *borrow* the wealth of their oppressors to aid in working their way from Egyptian bondage. The fathers of the revolution did not stand on etiquette at Bunker Hill, Saratoga or Yorktown, when striking for independence. But we in Kansas have allowed the enemy to coil his chain, link after link, around us; and we, with the dignity of injured innocence, have stood quiet and watched the progress of the work, until now the few last links are being laid, and the rivet is being prepared which shall fasten the work and leave us forever in his power.

"Freemen of Kansas! Do you not see the progress of the enslaver? The last hope is dying out! Another period lost, and we are *lost*—irrevocably lost.

"While the enemy has been at work, employing every artifice his ingenuity could invent, to perfect his work of crushing us, we have been hugging a delusive *phantom* to our bosoms—a phantom which has exhausted our best efforts to enfuse life into it, and yet it is a *phantom*. [Alluding to the Topeka Constitution.]

"The opportunity which, if improved, would have given us a controlling influence in the Constitutional Convention has been allowed to pass. Such was the decree of the Topeka Convention of March last. It was political heterodoxy to oppose its action. No Convention now binds our hands; and we wish to be understood as laying down a platform upon which *we* are going to stand, unless it is manifestly the will of a majority of the Free State party to occupy other grounds. In that case we shall sacrifice our private convictions to secure harmonius action.

"Our policy is this:

"*First*—If the Lecompton Constitution shall be submitted to a vote of the people, whether to those who are registered, or those who have been here three months, or six months, or any other period, we must vote, and vote it down. It matters not what the character of that Constitution may be. Though it is the Topeka Constitution itself, or one which is entirely unexceptionable, it is an exotic, foreign to our soil, imposed upon us by fraud, and it *must be voted down*.

"*Second*—Though the Constitution is not submitted to a vote of the people, or any part of them, we must take possession of it, and elect every officer, executive, legislative, and judical, under it; and although we cannot produce an abortion, we can *strangle* it at its birth, by getting possession of the *monster* when it begins to give evidence of life. Thus we can defeat our enemies in their scheme to trade off the freedom of Kansas to secure the admission of Minnesota into the Union.

"*Third*—We must elect a Territorial delegate to Congress, by claiming the application of the organic act to the election of that officer; and if this privilege is denied us, we must adopt the advice of a father to his son: 'Labor to get rich, honestly if you can, but by all means get rich.' Not that we advise dishonest means; but we must vote under bogus authority, if we cannot otherwise. At all events, we must elect the next delegate to Congress, and he must be a sterling man; one who has not been mixed up to too great an extent with our past troubles, but, nevertheless, one who is sufficiently known to the country to ensure a harmonious vote in his favor.

"*Fourth*—We must elect the next Territorial Legislature — not a part of it, but the whole. We have numbers sufficient to secure such a result in every election district, and will have hundreds to spare. To make the moral effect as complete as possible, it will be policy for all to vote, and thus secure the next Legislature in our own hands. This done, the whole bogus statutes should be erased by one act of the Legislature, and if vetoed by the Governor, it should be passed over his veto. Then a wise code of laws, such as is suited to our condition, should be passed, and then will commence our prosperity.

"*Fifth*—Congress should be petitioned for large grants of lands, which would place us on an equality with the most favored of the Territories. While we can draw nourishment from Uncle Sam to keep our government alive, we should continue our Territorial existence, and only seek to throw off our swaddling clothes, in time to entitle us to vote in 1860, for Presidential electors.

"*Sixth*—The Topeka Constitution, which was only brought forward as a means to enable Congress to help us out of our unpleasant position, having been virtually twice rejected by that body, will be allowed to go by default, without wasting further time or money trying to give it a galvanic life, lasting only while the wires are in direct contact with it.

*   *   *   *   *   *

"Thus much for *our* position. Without caring what the opinions of the New York *Tribune*, or the corps of Eastern correspondents may be in regard to it, we submit the whole to the honest consideration of the actual settlers of Kansas, and trust they will give it their impartial consideration. Our policy may not be the best, but we believe it the only one which will ensure the freedom of Kansas."

The publication of this leader, which contemplated a solution of our difficulties through a resort to the PEACEFUL ballot, and not by forcible resistance, aroused the animosity of the letter writers against the *Herald of Freedom* as never before. From that time forward, misrepresentation, calumny, and every species of vituperation, which Bohemian ingenuity and malice could invent were employed to crush the paper and its editor. No falsehood was too base to publish, no slander was too villainous to repeat, and as we look back through the long years since then, we confess a feeling of indignation that men so wholly destitute of truth or honorable impulses should have been allowed by respectable Eastern journalists, to transcend their vocation, to falsify and belittle those who were infinitely their superiors in every-thing that constituted genuine merit.*

*To illustrate the feelings of others in regard to our abuse by the letter-writers, we quote from that sterling Free State paper, a take-off, by Sol Miller, of the White Cloud Chief:

" We think certain Eastern journals and some in Kansas, that profess to have much concern for the welfare of the Territory, might do her far more service, if they would pay a little more

Referring to those slanders, and our position, in an editorial of date August 1, 1857, replying to the N. H. *Sentinel*, we said:

"We know our position is approved by a very large number of leading Republicans in the States, and a great majority of the Free State settlers in the Territory. It is a policy which will relieve us from our present difficulties, without resort to revolution, and will give freedom to Kansas, and all that unoccupied public domain lying north and west of us to the Pacific. With this knowledge we can afford to be misrepresented, slandered, anything, so we secure our aspirations in coming to Kansas."

The great mass of people were with us at the outset, and many of the public leaders occupied the same position, among whom I note with pleasure, Gov. CHAS. ROBINSON, though for reasons which will afterward appear, this was not known to the writer at the

attention to her real interests, and not quite so much to retailing silly stuff about G. W. BROWN, of the *Herald of Freedom*. There are correspondents of the St. Louis *Democrat*, Chicago *Tribune,* New York *Tribune*, and other *Tribunes*, whose main object, judging from their letters, seems to be to bark at Brown, who cannot blow his nose, spit on the sidewalk, or accidentally tread on a cat's tail, without they immediately post it off by express to their respective journals, as "Another Contemptible act of 'Gusty Windy' Brown," or something of that sort. And there are papers in the Territory silly enough to peddle out this trash here. What is the object of this? In what way does it affect the cause of Free Kansas, whether Brown eats onions for supper, wipes his nose on his coat sleeve, or wears a shirt six weeks without washing? To read some of the papers, one would think Brown's legs were a pro-slavery infernal machine, and that the seat of some obscure person's breeches were the nest wherein the Bird of Freedom has deposited her eggs, and that if the former came in contact with the latter a general smash-up of human liberty would ensue. Come, gentlemen, can't you be prevailed upon to 'Don't.'"

time, Gen. S. C. Pomeroy, Judge P. C. Schuyler,
Hon. G. W. Smith, C. K. Holliday, Marcus J. Parrott,
Joel K. Goodin, Gen. Thomas Ewing, C. V. Eskridge,
S. N. Wood, Dr. Jas. Davis, in short, a very large
majority of the leading, influential and substantial
citizens of the Territory. Of those known to the
public who violently opposed this program, until it
was adopted by the Free State party, in convention
at Grasshopper Falls, in August after, of which I
shall have occasion to mention at greater length, as
we advance, were P. B. Plumb, T. D. Thacher, Wm.
A. Phillips, Martin F. Conway, Richard Realf, John
E. Cook, R. J. Hinton, Jas. Redpath, and the whole
herd of professional letter-writers. Of Gen. Jas.
H. Lane, it is due to truth to state, that he opposed
the "voting policy" as it was called, until after his
arrival at Grasshopper Falls, when he surprised
everybody, friends and foes alike, to the great chagrin
of the former, by making a speech advocating the
measure. His opposers ascribed the sudden revolution in feeling and expression to the fact that he had
an earnest desire to be on the *winning side.* Perhaps
it is just to say of these "lunatics," as an Eastern
journalist very felicitiously termed those who were
opposed to voting, as soon as the party decided to
participate in the election they were the first to
demand the public offices. As the years have gone,
two of these "lunatics" have suicided, two have died on
the gallows, some have lingered for years, and others
have died in insane asylums, one is still connected
with the public press, while—most lamentable of all
—two have been elected to Congress, and three others
to the United States Senate.

CHAPTER IX.

Gov. Walker in a Rage.

THE INDEPENDENT charter of the city of
Lawrence, which originated with a few "uneasy
politicians," and which was generally repudiated by
the citizens as an illegitimate bantling, elected officers
under it on the 13th of July, the charter itself having been adopted on the 8th, less than one-third of
the voters in the city participating in the election.

On the morning of the election for officers under
the organization, Gov. Walker, in an army ambulance,
accompanied by Lieut. Carr, of the United States
army, arrived in Lawrence. The Lieutenant, who
acted in the capacity of Aid to the Governor, called
at the *Herald of Freedom* office, and stated that the
Governor wished to see the editor in his private room
at the Morrow House. The writer was conducted to
the Governor's room on the second floor in that cara-
vansary, and was received with much warmth by his
Excellency, Lieut. Carr retiring. After being seated
Gov. Walker began recounting a series of grievances
against the Free State party. He said the Topeka
party, late in session in a legislative capacity, had
attempted to pass a code of laws, and put them in
force in opposition to the Territorial laws, and to
their exclusion; that the more conservative of that
body had opposed such measures; then an effort was
made to organize counties and cities; that scheme

also failed as a legislative measure; but the people were advised to organize cities and counties, inde-dendent of any legislative action; in short were to do in detail what they dare not attempt as a whole; then with the machinery of government in operation in the principal localities of the Territory; they could set in motion their State machinery and run out the Terri-torial government. In furtherance of this movement he said Gen. Lane had asked for authority to organ-ize the Free State men in military companies, osten-sibly to protect the ballot-box, but his object was clearly to expel the Territorial government, and set in force, in defiance of law, the Topeka government.

The Governor seemed considerably excited while making his narration; called the acts "incipient rebel-lion," and said the thing must be put down. While he was yet talking, a young man entered the room, a stranger to the writer, who walked back and forth, evidently taking in the whole conversation. Gov. Walker seemed greatly nettled for a time, then sprang to his feet in great anger, and said:

"Mr. Brown, I have never come to this house since arriving in the Territory, but there have been spies upon my every movement. I feel perfectly outraged that I cannot talk with a friend without being sub-jected to such insolent surveillance. Go back to your office, and when I wish to see you again, I will call upon you at your own rooms. The people of Law-rence will have occasion to regret this insult."

I tried to interrupt the Governor, and to explain the condition of things, and show him that he was misinformed in regard to the action at Topeka, and

that the municipal movement was not an expression
of the popular will; that Mr. Morrow, the proprietor
of the hotel, was perfectly ignorant of the insults he
was receiving, but he cut me short, and, in a commanding tone and manner, bade me go away at once.
Not wishing to increase the storm, I obeyed, and from
the door of the *Herald of Freedom* building, a few
minutes after, saw Lieut. Carr drive in front of the
hotel with an ambulance, the Governor enter, and
start towards Leavenworth.

CHAPTER X.

THE NEXT thing we hear of Gov. Walker was on the following Thursday, the 16th of July, when a messenger arrived from Leavenworth, stating that Gov. Walker and a regiment of United States troops, with a battery, were moving on the town from the fort, and would reach us on the next day; that he had issued a proclamation directed to the people of Lawrence; its character was not well understood.

A meeting of the citizens was convened in front of the Morrow House that evening, when the matter was discussed, and a committee of five were appointed, consisting of G. W. Collamore, G. W. Brown, E. A. Coleman, A. H. Mallory and Charles Stearns, to wait on the Governor, and inquire of him if the proclamation was genuine, and his object in invading the city with a military force.

Friday morning the committee held a meeting. Messrs. Collamore and Brown were instructed to wait on the Governor, on his arrival, and learn when it would be convenient for him to receive the Committee.

The Governor, with his troops, crossed the river on the ferry, and passed through town, while the Committee were in a little controversy over some trifling matter of etiquette, Mr. Stearns being overruled in the premises. Mr. C. and myself followed

the troops, and found them erecting tents on the
prairie, about one-half mile west of the town. The
Governor received us very politely, invited us to seats
in his ambulance, and voluntarily gave us the reason
for his movement. We endeavored to disabuse his
mind of the false impressions he had formed; assured
him that the charter movement was the action of an
irresponsible faction, which we had been resisting as
illegal and outside of law; that it was merely boy's
play, and was so regarded by all our better citizens,
though the instigators of the movement had used the
names of several of our prominent citizens as officers,
merely to give it the appearance of respectability;
that he might as well hold the people responsible for
the action of a moot Legislature, as for such a body,
and their doings.

The Governor thanked us for the call, expressed
regret that he had taken such hasty action, said, if in
his interview with Mr. Brown on Monday morning he
had not been outraged and insulted by a system of
espionage, which always angered him, he should not
have acted so unwisely. We told him the object of
our visit, and wished to know when he would give the
committee a formal hearing. He named five o'clock
in the afternoon.

The committee, with the exception of Mr. Stearns,
who declined to act, met Gov. Walker at the hour designated, and the same subject was again canvassed,
but not so fully or freely as at the informal
meeting.

Gen. Lane and Gov. Robinson came down from
Topeka while Mr. Collamore and myself were with

the Governor. Mr. Stearns, a disunion abolitionist
of the Garrison school, made a prejudiced report to
these leaders, of what the committee proposed to do.
Another meeting was hastily called in the street, a
shameful misrepresentation of facts was made, and
the committee and their acts were repudiated. A
negro messenger on horseback met us on our way to
town from the camp, who handed us the repudiating
resolutions. Mr. Collamore, afterwards mayor of the
city, and a victim of the murderous Quantrell Raid
in August of 1863, was greatly outraged at Gen. Lane
because of this petty insult. The committee, nevertheless, discharged their duty faithfully; reported
their interview with the Governor in writing, to an
adjourned meeting of the citizens on Saturday evening, and received the thanks of the people for their
action.

Capt. Samuel Walker, one of the bravest and most
trusty of our Free State leaders, informed the writer
that as Mr. Collamore and myself left camp, at the
informal interview, he entered it, and met Gov.
Walker, who grasped his hand and arm with both
hands, and said: "Captain, I have acted hastily and
unadvisedly in bringing these troops here. You must
aid me in getting out of this difficulty."

The proclamation was a bombastic document,
wholly unworthy the head and heart of so distinguished a gentleman as Gov. Walker. Reading it
over as we write, we do not wonder the letter-writers
made mirth of it, or that a fictitious proclamation
was issued, filled with "blood and thunder." How
the Governor could wade through nearly two columns
of a newspaper, "imploring the people to not compel

him to use the military power," and "adjuring them
to abandon their unlawful proceedings before involving themselves in the crime of treason," is certainly
unaccountable on any other hypothesis than that he
was simply "luny" when he wrote it. I make the following extract from a letter of his, written at Leavenworth, before marching on Lawrence, addressed to the
Secretary of State at Washington, quoted by President Buchanan in a special message to Congress on
Kansas affairs, dated Feb. 2, 1858:

"The movement at Lawrence was the beginning of a
plan originating in that city; to organize an insurrection throughout the Territory, and especially in all
the towns, cities and counties where the Republican
party have a majority. Lawrence is the hot-bed of
all abolition movements in this Territory. It is the
idea established by the Abolition societies of the
East, and whilst there are a number of respectable
people there, it is filled by a considerable number of
mercenaries, who are paid by the Abolition societies
to perpetuate and diffuse agitation throughout Kansas, and prevent the peaceful settlement of this question. Having failed in inducing their now so-called
Topeka State Legislature to organize this insurrection, Lawrence has commenced it herself, and if not
arrested, rebellion will extend throughout the Territory. * * The continued presence of Gen. Harney
is indispensable, as was originally stipulated by me,
with a large body of dragoons and several batteries."

In an editorial published by us, with the proclamation, and immediately following it, we said:

"We regret this act on the part of Gov. Walker, as
its tendency is to inflame the people at a time when
all parties should be laboring to establish an era of
peace. We have no sympathy with the independent
city organization, as was indicated in our last number,

rp 69td ei1p

it r

ps

and greatly regretted it, as we were apprehensive it would bring upon us just what seems rapidly approaching. While we take exceptions to that movement, we also take exceptions to Gov. Walker bringing the military to Lawrence. If he had legal process to serve, it should have been served by United States authority, and no man in Lawrence or out of it, would have resisted. Our people—all of them, the extremists included—know too well that Uncle Sam's authority is not to be opposed with impunity.

"Gov. Walker may send troops here, and may arrest those connected with the organization of the City Government. This is all he can accomplish. There will be no resistance, hence no bloodshed. ⋅ Matters will move on quietly, and the agitators on either side will not be able to get up a serious collision.

"We hope Gov. Walker will not allow bad counsels to govern him in this crisis. He is surrounded by men who desire to drive our people into extreme measures; but we are conscious the Free State party is occupying high vantage ground, and we shall not be driven from it, by sustaining extreme measures on the one hand or resisting federal authority on the other. The policy of our people and Gov. Walker is identical, as shadowed in his speech at Topeka, the first, to preserve the quiet of the Territory, 'peaceably if we can, but at all events to preserve the general quiet;' secondly, for the people to get the Territorial government into their own hands, and administer it for the benefit of the actual residents.

"This being the case, it is the interest of Gov. Walker as well as the people, to keep agitating questions out of sight, and avoid every movement which tends to acerbation on either hand. The bringing of troops to Lawrence cannot be viewed in any other light than to overawe and intimidate the people, and induce them to acquiesce in the plans of the Governor. He may succeed in convincing the South, that he is true to his first love, but he cannot succeed in subjugating the people of Lawrence, or of the Territory."

CHAPTER XI.

Danger Averted.

THE PEOPLE of Lawrence and the whole country were greatly excited over Gov. Walker's movement with the troops. Every sort of wild rumor immediately filled the air, and was sent to the States by letters and telegrams. Hardly an hour passed but parties were calling on the editor of the Herald of Freedom for explanation of the affair. Those who had been so violent in their denunciations of the paper and its editor were still more denunciatory, and Eastern papers joined in the "hue and cry" until the very atmosphere seemed hazed with their bitterness. A few silly patrons in the States sent back their papers with insulting indorsements upon them. The Free State papers which had opposed Gov. Walker from the beginning renewed their hostility and violent abuse of that functionary. The Governor became enraged, and threats of vengeance were reported as coming from him. I became alarmed myself, fearful that the calumnious charges against the Governor and his friends, would defeat all our hopes. Filled with these emotions, and recalling my first interview with him, I wrote the following, and passed a copy of it to the printers to put in type, reserving the original for my own use. Telling my associate editor, Mr. Wattles, my purpose to visit the military camp, I took my way there alone.

Entering Col. Cook's camp, and learning which

was the Governor's tent, I made my way to it. Governor Walker came out of the tent as I neared it, and, unlike his usual cordiality and open hand, with a generous warmth of expression, extended only his index finger. I received it with a full hand, announced my business to read him an editorial, already in type for the next number of my paper, in regard to him. He thanked me for calling, brought camp stools from the tent, and we took seats near the front of the tent. I then read him the following, published verbatim as written, in my issue of August 1st, headed:

"LIES NAILED.—It is false that Gov. Walker has said he will interfere with the election of State officers, under the Topeka Constitution on Monday next. On the contrary, he has repeatedly stated he would not forcibly interfere with the carrying out of measures for the preservation of the State organization, so far as contemplates an application to Congress for admission into the Union under the Constitution.

"It is false that Gov. Walker has declared it his intention to call upon Missouri for volunteers to aid him in any event in his Kansas mission. He has always said if military power is required to preserve the peace of the Territory, he would call to his aid the United States troops, which are, or may be subject to his orders.

"It is false that the Governor brought the troops to Lawrence, with a view to the collection of taxes; on the contrary, his object was expressed in his proclamation, which we published last week, which all men can read at their leisure.

"It is false that Gov. Walker has at any time stated that the voters in the election of October next will be limited to those who were registered under the last census act. He has declared repeatedly that no such legislation shall be imposed upon voters; and this he asserted publicly in his speech at Big Springs, in June last, in reply to interrogatories propounded to him at that time.

"It is false that the Governor brought the troops to Lawrence with the view of embroiling the people, and demolishing the town; on the contrary, he will labor to prevent such a catastrophe, having in view only the arrest of the officers under the municipal organization, should they proceed to complete the organization under the independent charter.

"It is true Gov. Walker has declared to all persons with whom he has discoursed on the subject, that he will preserve the quiet of the Territory at whatever cost; and will call the entire force of the United States troops at his command, to aid in preventing a reign of terror in Kansas, if their services are necessary."

The Governor listened attentively until I reached the conclusion, when, taking the manuscript in his hand and glancing over it, he said: "All very well, Mr. Brown, but you will have to amend the third paragraph by inserting after 'taxes,' *but circumstances have occurred since his arrival here which render it probable he will employ them in this direction.*" He then went on to say that the Sheriff had only a few days before called on Wm. Jesse, at Bloomington, to assess taxes; that Jesse caught a carpenter's adz near him, and ran the Sheriff off his premises. "The Sheriff has called on me for troops to aid him, and I see no other way than to furnish them."

"Governor, that would be in violation of your agreement made with me at our first interview. You said, as you will well recollect, that you would refuse to aid in the collection of taxes until after the October election, in consideration of the people participating in the Territorial elections. This editorial was written, predicated on that agreement, and I cannot consent to alter it in a single word."

"Then it will not agree with the facts."

"I give the article based upon your solemn agreement. If you have changed your purpose it is not to be presumed I know anything about it. If you act differently from what you promised, I shall tell my readers of the pledge you made me at our first interview; that in consequence of that pledge I have thus far sustained Gov. Walker's policy; that as he has broken faith with me I am no longer under obligations to him, and that I cannot sustain his administration any farther. You know the fact, Governor, that I had over 8,000 subscribers to my paper when I commenced endorsing you. I have lost a good many subscribers because of that support. Life-long friends, whom I esteemed highly, have listened to the falsehoods of your enemies, and have arrayed themselves against me. If, however, you do as you promised, the result will be satisfactory; the people will see that I was right, and that those who opposed me were wrong, and all will be well in the end; but if you go back on your promises, I shall put myself right before the public by showing that it is you who have broken faith in the premises."

"You can show the public how I have been driven into this measure by the violent action of your people, and you can set yourself right with the public in that way."

"Governor, I shall abide by my agreement with you to the letter, and if you break it I shall act accordingly."

The conversation was somewhat lengthy, but all in

the direction indicated. I arose, bade the Governor good day, and started on my return. Perhaps a couple of rods away, he called me back, bade Lieutenant Carr, who first put in an appearance at this point, to bring out a bottle of wine and two glasses. The Governor opened the bottle and said:

"Mr. Brown, take a glass of wine with me."

"I never drink wine, Governor."

"Never drink wine? Well, I take a glass of Maderia occasionally. What will you take?"

"A glass of cold water, please, I never take anything stronger."

"You are rather puritanical, Mr. Brown."

Again the proposed change in the editorial was talked over. Again I answered him that it would appear as written; again bade him good day, and returned to my office. The article appeared in my Saturday's issue unchanged. Gov. Walker did not employ the troops to aid in the collection of taxes; indeed there was never any further effort in that direction; and thus another source of danger—that threatened by Secretary Stanton when he first entered the Territory, and which the pro-slavery element had labored so hard to bring about, with the hope of bringing on another collision with the authorities— was turned aside.

When in Kansas in September, 1880, I told Col. Samuel Walker, one of the first Free State settlers in the Territory, and now a resident of Lawrence, of this interview. In giving the words of the Governor, he added to my narrative additional remarks of the Governor. "True," I replied, "but how did you know this?"

"I heard the whole conversation between you and the Governor."

"Is that possible? Where were you?"

"I was in the Governor's tent; had called to talk with him on the same subject. Our conversation was interrupted by your appearance. I was reclining upon his lounge, separated from you by the cloth tent only. After you left, and the Governor entered the tent, he said: 'That Brown is a remarkable person. He will not swerve a hair's breadth from his position. He even refused a glass of wine with me.' You lost nothing in your influence with the Governor by your firmness to principle on that occasion."*

Whatever may have been Gov. Walker's *real* motive in stationing a regiment of United States troops near Lawrence; thence to Fort Riley, on the 3d of August, and back to the vicinity of Lecompton, it was clearly apparent that the Governor felt greatly annoyed when the President ordered the return of the troops to Fort Leavenworth. He left Lecompton and accompanied them to their old quarters, where he remained for several weeks, the report being current that he had resigned and left the Territory in disgust. Indeed, if I remember rightly, he spent nearly all his time at

*Col. Samuel Walker, one of the first settlers in 1854 in the vicinity of Lawrence, was born in Pennsylvania in 1823, and died at Lawrence on February 6, 1893. He was an active worker in the Free State ranks; commanded a regiment in the war of the Rebellion, served several terms in the State Legislature, and was always faithful to duty. He was breveted Brigadier General for distinguished services against the Sioux Indians. A letter from the Colonel, indorsing the above statements, will be found in the Appendix.

the Fort from then until immediately after the October election.

CHAPTER XII.

Preparing for the Contest.

FREE STATE CONVENTION was held at Topeka, on the 15th and 16th of July, 1857, to nominate candidates for the offices under the Topeka Constitution, the term being near the close for which the officers were elected in 1855. At this July Convention the question of participating in the Territorial election in October was discussed at considerable length. Conventions, mass and delegate, were finally provided for, to assemble at Grasshopper Falls, on the last Wednesday in August, "to take such action as may be deemed necessary with regard to the election." A resolution was also adopted, on motion of M. F. Conway, who was identified with the "fighting policy," as it was called in contradistinction to the "voting policy," authorizing "Gen. Jas. H. Lane to organize the people of the Territory into military districts, etc., to protect the ballot-boxes at the approaching election in Kansas." This resolution was a favorite project of Gen. Lane and his endorsers, at the Convention, and as an *attempt* was afterwards made on two occasions to use the forces thus organized for serious disturbing purposes we here, in passing, call attention to the *public source* of his power.

In the interim, between the Topeka Convention, and the assembling at Grasshopper Falls, the contest between the opposing factions of the Free State party were more bitter than at any other period. The correspondents of the Eastern press were ubiquitous. They forced themselves into every private caucus, and attempted to control it by their votes; then, through their respective journals, denounced those of opposing views in unmeasured terms, who generally triumphed with the people. We recall two or three of these district conventions—one at Centropolis, on the 14th of August, at which the letter-writers were present in full force, with a considerable number of their endorsers. A dinner—more properly a barbecue—was furnished by the citizens, of which the correspondents participated. They then falsely reported to their respective journals, that "Gov. Walker contributed $500 to get up the dinner." Notwithstanding their hostility, resolutions were adopted by less than a dozen opposing votes determining to participate in all future Territorial elections. One was held at Judge Spicer's, a few miles west of Lawrence, called by the voting element. This was taken possession of by their Free State opponents, and they absolutely elected Gen. Maclean, a most violent pro-slavery leader, residing at Lecompton, and afterwards known to the country as "the candle-box conspirator," chairman of the meeting. After making a denunciatory pro-slavery speech, Maclean had the good sense to decline the duty. The discussion which followed greatly revolutionized the general feeling in favor of those who called the convention.

Large meetings were also held at Willow Springs; at Rockingham, in Pottawatomie county; on South Pottawatomie Creek, in Anderson county; at Sugar

Creek, in Linn county; and, indeed, all over the Territory, all indorsing the voting policy.

The general convention, at Grasshopper Falls, on the 26th of August, was fully represented by the people. The mass convention, in which all participated, was designed to adopt a policy for the government of the party; while the delegate convention would nominate a candidate for delegate to Congress, in case the mass convention deemed it advisable to contest the Territorial elections.

The men engaged in stirring up strife were there; but it was soon apparent the people were determined to try the peaceful ballot. They reasoned that if they went into the election and were defeated by fraud or by violence they could go before the country and Congress with their grievances, with some hope of redress; while, if they remained silent and inactive, the proslavery party would elect their candidates for offices again without opposition, probably using neither fraud nor violence, hence, because of our apathy they would have an easy victory; that our friends in the States would be disgusted at our neglect to grasp the favorable opportunity when we could have regained our rights. M. F. Conway, Wm. A. Phillips, P. B. Plumb, Jas. Redpath, and T. D. Thatcher, led the opposition to the voting policy. Arrayed against them were the substantial leaders of the Free State party, among whom, well-known to the public, we note with pleasure the names of Chas. Robinson, G. W. Smith, W. Y. Roberts, C. K. Holliday, Robert Morrow, S. C. Pomeroy, F. A. Adams, Dr. Jas. Davis, P. C. Schuyler, etc. Gen. Lane was opposed to taking any part in the October elections, even declaring

to the committee on resolutions, of which he was a
member, that it was impracticable to do so.   He, however, afterwards made an earnest speech in favor of
that policy.   Gov. Robinson spoke at considerable
length in favor of that measure.   He compared the
bogus laws to a battery which had been playing with
shot and shell on the Free State party.   He was in
favor of turning it on our enemies, also making it
ineffectual by spiking it.   Characteristic of the opposition, a voice in the crowd cried out, "He has sold
himself to Gov. Walker."

On motion of the writer, the resolutions reported
by the business committee, in favor of voting, were
adopted by acclamation.   In the reported proceedings, I find the following paragraph:

"James Redpath, from the stand, addressing G. W.
Brown, said: '*Your policy has prevailed!* You have
triumphed! and the people are evidently with you.
You have been assailed from all quarters, but the people have taken their position on your platform, as
appears by the action of this convention.'"

Marcus J. Parrott was put in nomination as delegate to Congress; and after electing a new Territorial
Committee, of which the writer continued one, the
convention closed in harmony, having

Resolved, That we, the people of Kansas, in mass
convention assembled, agree to participate in the
October election; that in thus acting we rely upon the
faithful fulfilment of the pledges of Gov. Walker;
and that we, as heretofore, protest against the enact-
ments forced upon us by the voters of Missouri.

The bogus Legislature, at its last session, repealed
the law requiring a test oath and a dollar tax to be
paid by each voter.   They also made provision for the

election of a new legislature; requiring the Governor to make an apportionment by the first day of June. Failing to do so, the President of the Council, and Speaker of the House were required to make such apportionment by the middle of the month. The manuscript laws were sent to St. Louis to be printed, and as the Governor never knew of their provisions he failed to comply with them, hence the pro-slavery heads of the House and Council made the apportionment, and so gerrymandered every Representative and Council district as to connect the interior districts save one, *with a county bordering on Missouri.* Such districts, however distant, in one case reaching to the summit of the Rocky Mountains, had a voting precinct easily accessible by those who had heretofore done our voting for us. Some of the counties composing the districts were not even contiguous, but were separated more than fifty miles from their associated counties. An appeal was made to Gov. Walker to correct the apportionment, but he was powerless to act; so the election was forced upon us, with all these terrible disadvantages.

CHAPTER XIII.

The Election and Fictitious Returns.

WE HAVE now reached the most important epoch in Kansas history, and one the future historian will find full of thrilling incidents, for on it hinges the destiny of an institution whose beginning antedates the oldest human records,— whose end in Republican America, and, by reflex action, throughout the civilized world—though effaced with an ocean of blood, is clearly traceable to that period when the Free State party triumphed at the polls at the October election of 1857, obtained control of the law-making power, and wielded it for freedom against their oppressors. Not that our victory was complete, for we shall observe, before closing these chapters, as soon as one danger was removed, we were beset by another, and still another, until the hopes of many failed them.

The Grasshopper Falls' convention united the antagonistic elements of the Free State party, the conservative element of it very generally subordinating their claims to the public offices to the more radical wing, to the end that there should be no cause for further division.

The pro-slavery party seemed inactive. No fears were entertained of a general invasion from Missouri; that if attempted at all, it would be limited to the polling precincts on the border, through which they would secure further control of the legislative power. It was believed they were so confident of being admitted into the Union under the Constitution, then in progress of formation, they would not care to incur the trouble and expense of electing a Territorial Legislature. Each party, however, entered the canvass with a full ticket.

Gov. Walker, on the 16th of September, published a letter, in the nature of a proclamation to the people, occupying seven full columns closely set, in the Herald of Freedom, in which he reviewed the law govering the election. In closing he declared, in substance, which we somewhat abridge:

"However solicitous I may be about the result of the pending election, or anxious, those views of public policy which I have entertained and expressed from my youth up, especially as regards the EQUILIBRIUM of our government, should triumph in October, *yet I cannot and will not do any act, or countenance or sustain any, the effect of which will deprive the people of Kansas of any rights secured to them by the federal compact, the organic act, or the laws of the Territory.*"

The Governor stated in this letter that the troops at his command would be placed in the neighborhoods of election precincts where violence or outrage on the ballot-box was apprehended, on request of either party, "not for the purpose of overawing the people, or of interfering in any way with the elections, but, by their mere presence, guarding the polls against attempts at insurrection or violence."

The election was held on Monday, October 5th. The day was wet and cheerless, while previous protracted rains had made the mud deep and the traveling difficult. The polls were few, and the people, other than residents of towns, had to make long journeys to exercise the right of suffrage. Besides, it was at the season of the year when there was much sickness in the Territory. From these and other causes, it was estimated one-fourth of the Free State vote was lost; nevertheless, as the returns arrived from distant points, it was evident the Free State candidates were elected by handsome majorities.

When we were triumphing over the result news arrived, first, that 500 votes were polled at the pro-slavery town of Kickapoo, on the Missouri river opposite Weston, Mo., by which the Leavenworth district, with its eight members in the House and three in the Council were given to the pro-slavery party. It was well known this vote was almost wholly fraudulent or simulated; but the next question was how to controvert it.

Then came a report that Oxford, an insignificant point, directly across the Territorial line from Little Santa Fe, Mo., without half a dozen legal voters, had returned 1,626 votes. This precinct was attached to the Lawrence district, and these simulated votes, if counted, would overcome the heavy Free State vote, and give eight more pro-slavery members to the House and three to the Council, united with the Leavenworth district and the Legislature would again be in the hands of the enemies of freedom.

And then from McGee county there were returns of some 1,200 votes, while there was not a legal voter in the county, it being Indian territory, and not open to settlement, "exempted out of and forming no part of the Territory of Kansas," by express provision of the organic act. If these simulated returns were counted by the Governor and Secretary, not only would the Legislative Assembly remain in pro-slavery hands, but so would the delegate to Congress, and most of the county officers.

The excitement of the people became almost violent. To add to its intensity—as it was well known Gov. Walker was at Fort Leavenworth at the time of the election—it was reported he was appealed to on the day of election, and decided that soldiers stationed at the Fort had a legal right to vote, and, in consequence, they had exercised the franchise and swelled the opposition.

The Free State military organizations were aroused into activity; a small party of armed men set out for Oxford to make observations, and learn the facts which transpired at that precinct, and the names of the scoundrels who were the perpetrators of the fraud. Threats of assassination of the Territorial officers were rife, and those who had been most earnest in supporting the voting policy, were the most bitter in their determination to thwart the outrage by fair means or foul.

The writer was waited upon by a committee of three prominent gentlemen of Lawrence, and requested to visit Lecompton, see the Governor, present the condition of affairs to him, and induce him, if possible, to reject those fictitious returns. It was urged that it was through the instrumentality of the Herald of Freedom the people had participated in the election; that reposing confidence in Gov. Walker's pledges, guaranteeing a fair and honest election, the result

had been brought about; they tendered a span of
horses and carriage, with D. W. Wier, Esq., a young
lawyer then resident of Lawrence, for company on
condition I would go.

A paper was drawn up, reciting the facts in regard
to the frauds, signed by thirty well known citizens,
who made oath before a Notary to the truth of the
statements. They solemnly protested against these
returns being counted.

It was reported the Governor returned to Lecompton the day before and immediate action was necessary. It was near sundown when we set out on our
mission, probably on the 14th of October, for that
was the date of the protest.

Lecompton had no particular charms for us. We
had first visited it on the 20th of May, 1856, under
duress, guarded by a body of horsemen commanded
by Col. Titus, at last advices an incurable paralytic of
Titusville, Florida, the redoubtable pro-slavery ruffian, who was afterwards connected with the Nica-
ragua expedition, commanded by "Fillibuster
Walker." For nearly four months we had been held
a prisoner, with others, in that vicinity. Whenever
the name was mentioned the bitter sarcasm of Judge
Smith, a fellow prisoner, semi-delirious with chills
and fever, would come to mind: "Hell is just over
the hill yonder. I get the sulphurous odor every
time I turn my head that way. Don't you smell it!"
When we first came to the town it was filled with
Southern ruffians, hundreds of whom had gathered there preparatory to a descent on Lawrence on
the following day, to destroy our printing office, with

that of Messrs. Miller & Elliott's, and the Free State Hotel. On entering Lecompton on that occasion the streets were filled with the cowardly desperadoes, who, as we passed, cried out: "There is that G—d d—d Abolitionist Brown, of the Herald of Freedom. Shoot him! Shoot him! Why don't you shoot the d—d nigger thief? Loan me a gun, and I'll shoot him." These and similar expressions, always well mixed with oaths, were heard continually until we reached the quarters assigned us. Reader, do you wonder we call these bravos "cowardly," who treated a prisoner, unarmed and wholly in their power, in this shameful manner? Or that we never had any love for Lecompton or its pro-slavery inhabitants thereafter? And is it strange that the incidents of our first visit there were recalled on the occasion of our second, some thirteen months after our release without trial? Hon. Wm. H. Seward, in a speech at Lawrence, a couple of years later, emphasized Lecompton as "A forlorn widow, sitting there alone in her desolation." Even her "Lane University" will hardly save her from oblivion.

A part of the traveled road to Lecompton was unknown to us, and as it was only starlight, we lost our way, and brought up at Big Springs. Returning to Judge Wakefield's, and the night being so far spent, we tarried until morning. Renewing our journey at dawn, the incidents of our former journey to Lecompton, as just narrated, were vividly recalled.

It seemed as if our detention *en route* was providential, for the Governor only arrived at Lecompton about two o'clock in the morning from Ft. Leavenworth. It is probable, had we met with no delay, we should have missed an interview with him.

After breakfast, I sent my card to the Governor's room, who boarded at the same hotel where we stopped. No attention was paid to it. Waiting an hour or two, a second card was sent up requesting an interview; a third; dinner; and no attention to my cards. About two o'clock, Lieut. Carr, the Governor's Aid, presented himself, and said the Governor was very busy; that he was having an interview in his room with several gentlemen, and that it would be impossible for him to see me before three o'clock.

At three o'clock, I presented myself at his door, and was invited to his room, where, I should suppose, were from ten to a dozen well known pro-slavery men, who seemed in earnest conversation as I entered. The Governor invited me to a seat. I stated that I wished to see him alone, on important matters. He replied that he was busy, but would give me his first leisure moment. A short time passed, when Lieut. Carr announced the Governor was alone, and would give me a hearing. I went to his room again, when, casting about me, I said:

"Governor, my mission to you to-day is of a very important character, and it is with you alone. These walls, I observe, are of a kind that ears may be all around us. I wish to see you where we shall not be interrupted, and where there will be no reporters for either of us."

"We can go to the Executive Office," was his reply.

"Anywhere so we can be wholly alone, and where neither of us can be reported by others to our prejudice."

Together we went to the second story of a building a little distance away, which, though I had never entered before, from its surroundings was evidently his office. Giving me a chair, and taking one himself near by, he said:

"Here there are no ears to listen, and I have bolted the door so there will be no intrusion. Proceed with what you would say."

CHAPTER XIV.

Important Interview with Governor Walker.

"GOVERNOR, I have called to talk with you in regard to our present political condition. You are aware the people are worked up to fever heat over the fraudulent returns which have been sent to the Executive office from various election precincts, particularly from Oxford, in Johnson county, and those from McGee county, as also from Kickapoo."

"What evidence have you Mr. Brown, that those returns are fraudulent, as you allege?"

"Simply because we know there is no such population in the districts. Johnson county, in which this populous city is located, has been open to settlement only about six months, the length of time a person must have been a resident in the Territory to entitle him to a vote. Oxford is only separated from Little Santa Fe, Mo., by the Territorial line. There are not half a dozen houses in the town, and, probably, not fifty inhabitants all told in the precinct; and yet 1,626 votes are returned as cast there at the recent election. On the first day of the election we have positive proof that only ninety names were entered on the poll books when closed for the night, leaving 1,536 to be polled on the second day, a thing practically impossible, even had the voters all been formed in line, and each moment had been employed in receiving the ballots and entering names."

"Well, what do you say of McGee county?"

"That McGee county is Indian territory, not open to settlement, and there cannot be a legal vote there."

"But election precincts were provided for."

"By some person who was ignorant of the condition of the country, else with the design of paving the way to the fraud they have attempted to consummate."

"What of Kickapoo?"

"It is an unimportant town on the Missouri river, above Leavenworth, with not two hundred inhabitants, men, women and children in the precinct."

"Yes, we have received returns from these places you mention. The polls were opened in due form, at the time provided for by law; the returns are strictly formal; certified to by the officers authorized to hold the election; they are found correct in every respect."

"But nevertheless fraudulent."

"We have no means to determine that. The signatures of the officers seem genuine, and we have not been clothed with authority to go behind the returns, and inquire what transpired prior to the making up of the record."

"What did you mean then, Governor, by your promise to give us a fair and impartial election?"

"Simply just what I said. Has any man been deprived of his vote who was legally entitled to cast one? Have any polls been closed before the hour when they should have been closed? Tell me wherein you have not had a fair and impartial election."

"We do not complain of the election, but of the fictitious returns. It is to the counting of these to which we enter our protest."

"If the Legislature had given us power to go beyond

the returns, and inquire into the objections you urge
we would cheerfully do so, but we are as powerless as
you are in the premises."

"Governor, in our first interview, you said, had you
been in Gov. Reeder's place you would have suffered
the loss of your right arm, and been bored through
by a bullet before you would have given certificates
of election to those persons elected by non-residents
on the 30th of March, '55."

"And so I would. The cases are not parallel. Here
everything is formal."

"And everything was formal there."

"Then Reeder had no right to go behind the returns.
He acted in harmony with all the precedents in Legislative bodies, and even in Congress."

"They do it, nevertheless."

"A usurpation of power not conferred upon them
by the constitution."

"You are greatly disappointing us by your actions,
and placing those who relied upon your promises in a
very awkward dilemma."

"I am sorry if any one supposed I would violate
the law to carry a point against my own party."

"We supposed in your official action you would
stand above party."

"And so I have and will. But I will not strain a
point against my own convictions. My party friends
in the South have denounced me in unmeasured terms
because of my faithful discharge of duty; and the
radicals of Kansas and of the whole country have
assailed me constantly ever since I came here. Even
the Leavenworth *Times*, the other day, gave me a
column and a half of personal abuse. You have

always treated me courteously and kindly, but I suppose if my official action in this case does not meet your approbation, you, too, will not be sparing of denunciations."

"From your first arrival in Kansas, Governor, I have endeavored to do justly by you. Wherein I have differed from you I have not hesitated to say so; but never in a vindictive, malevolent spirit. You are well aware that my pecuniary loss, because of this action, must be measured by thousands of dollars. If you go back on your pledges, as we understand them, the Herald of Freedom may as well close its existence, unless I can regain my position by out-Heroding Herod. The truth is, those of your friends who place confidence in you—all of us—are compelled to take a public stand against you or go under."

"Be it so, then, but I shall discharge my duty faithfully."

"And count those fraudulent returns?"

"Count any returns that come to us properly authenticated with the signatures of the judges of the election, provided they are otherwise formal."

And thus point after point was introduced, and each was met firmly but courteously by the Governor. When every other resource seemed exhausted, I thought to try still another, a last resort, but was doubtful of its effect. Said I:

"Governor, before leaving there is a fact perhaps I ought, as your friend, to communicate to you; and yet it will cost me my life if it should be known to my party friends.

"What is it?"

"I will only communicate it to you on condition you will treat all I shall say as a profound secret—tell it to no one, and take no action, official or otherwise, to thwart it."

"You do not expect me to make you such a pledge?"

"Then you do not expect me to communicate a secret to you to save your life!"

"Is it of such a serious nature?"

"More so. It involves every government official in Kansas, and the stability of the Union itself!"

"What is it? Lose no time in telling it all."

"Only on condition of your solemn pledge as indicated."

"I give it."

"That you will not communicate to any one what I shall tell you, and that you will take no official or other action to prevent or defeat the plans, save as regards your own life."

"Yes."

"Do you know there is a secret Free State organization permeating this Territory, with a membership considerably exceeding ten thousand?"

"I have been told so."

"Were not the facts established by the report of the Congressional Investigation Committee in 1856?"

"Yes; the numbers were not given, but it was understood the membership was very large."

"And most thoroughly armed?"

"That is the understanding."

"And that they are acting in concert with the Republican party in the States, who will sustain this organization to the bloody issue?"

"I believe it."

[I was very glad he did, for I believed but a very small portion of it.]

"When I left Lawrence last night the people were in a perfect furor of excitement. They were organizing companies, one of which was about to proceed to Oxford to arrest the perpetrators of those villainous returns. It was proposed to execute every Territorial officer, and some were even desperate enough to favor a collision with the federal government if it stands in the way."

The Governor sprang to his feet in wild excitement, caught his hat, and said he would put a stop to such proceedings at once.

"Your pledge of honor, Governor, to take no action, official or otherwise, on any information I may impart to you."

"I will take measures to learn these facts from other sources.

"There will be no action save organization, and no movement of the company already in search of Batt Jones and his associates, until my return to Lawrence. Sit down; and let us talk these matters over."

He did so, and inquired: "Who are these conspirators?"

"They are not conspirators, Governor; They are freemen who know their rights and dare maintain them. The leaders are your best friends."

"And who are they?"

"Col. Eldridge, Robert Morrow, Jas. Blood, Judge Smith, Capt. Walker."

"You don't say that Capt. Walker is false to me?"

"No, he is true as steel, and will stand by and defend you to the last moment; but if you go back on your

pledge, he and Col. Eldridge, with every other conservative in the Territory, will take an open stand
against you."

"What can I do?"

"Redeem your pledges, and every conservative will
die in your defense, if need be."

"But your people have abused and falsified me
shamefully."

"This has all come from the radical element, who
have sought to involve the country in strife, hoping
to bring on a general war, to end in the dissolution
of the Union and of American slavery."

"Yes, and they will accomplish their wicked and
treasonable purposes unless arrested in their mad
schemes."

"You can arrest their plans by doing justly by the
people."

"Suppose I reject these returns as simulated and
fictitious, what will you do for me?"

"Anything you demand."

"Will you set me right before the people?"

"Most assuredly I will."

"And will you correct those damnable lies which
they have been repeating about me, even stating that
Gov. Walker changed clothes with a soldier at the
Fort, and then went up to the polls and voted the
pro-slavery ticket throughout, and advised everybody
else to do so?"

"Of course I will."

"And you will go to Lawrence and stop the insane
action of these men, who would engage in wholesale
murder and pillage; who would break up the govern-

ment and involve all the States in a general war?"

"I can promise you, Governor, that all this is contingent on your action."

"And you know there is no such population as the Oxford and McGee county returns indicate?"

"I have so officially certified in my *jurat*,attached as Notary to the protests against your and Secretary Stanton counting these returns."

"Will you write your next leader for the Herald of Freedom here, and allow me to dictate it?"

"I will."

"And, Mr. Brown, I am frank to say that I have some political aspirations of my own, after Kansas is admitted a State into the Union. My people in the South have gone back on me, and my future hope of position rests with the people of Kansas. Will you aid me with your paper?"

"When we are admitted a State under other than the proposed Lecompton constitution, if there is any place in the government you wish, from United States Senator down, if I can aid you to it, it is yours."

The Governor produced some paper, placed pen and ink before me, and said: "Write as I dictate." He folded his arms, and commenced walking back and forth, the length of the room, on the opposite side of the table from which I sat, reciting slowly, with lengthy pauses, as if reading from a book. Turn, reader, if accessible, to the Herald of Freedom of October 17th, 1857, copies of which are on file with the Historical Society, at Topeka, Kansas; with the Antiquarian Society, of Worcester, Mass.; in the State Library of New York; and, through the polite-

ness of the honorable Secretary of the Historical
Society of Kansas, a copy is temporarily in the writer's possession, while these sheets are being prepared; and on the second page, read the first article
headed: "Complicity of Gov. Walker in the Election
Frauds," filling two and one-fourth columns. That
article, every paragraph, sentence, line, and *even punctuation mark*, was dictated by Gov. Walker in the
manner indicated. When done, he said: "Read it
over carefully, and repeat the punctuation marks." I
did so. He said: "It is correct. And you will make
that article your leader in the next issue of your
paper?"

"I will."

"On Monday morning Secretary Stanton and I will
go down to Oxford, and see the country for ourselves.
Unless it is clear they have a population on which to
base such a vote, the returns from there shall be
rejected. Go back to Lawrence and assure your
friends that all will be well; that Gov. Walker will
keep faith with the people of Kansas; that he will
not go back on any of his pledges. Restrain them
from any acts of violence, and advise me if there is
danger of any further disturbance."

Thus, reader, I have detailed to you the substance
of an interview lasting from six to seven hours with
Gov. Walker, and though it may be I was induced to
promise what I would not, under other circumstances,
yet the consideration was great, involving results that
no one then dreamed of. We shook hands, bade each
other good night, and I made my way to the street.

Here is that editorial dictated by Gov. Walker. Its
publication was advised by Hon. Eli Thayer, after

reading the newspaper edition of these Reminiscences:

COMPLICITY OF GOV. WALKER IN ELECTION FRAUDS.—
Among the multiplicity of reports hourly reaching us of frauds in the late elections, the interference of Missourians, soldiers voting, and other grave charges against GOV. WALKER, we have thought it but just to the Governor and the public that we should inquire into them, and give our readers the result of our own investigations. Our purpose has been to arrive at the *truth*, not to shield the Governor, or any person acting in concert with him from deserved censure.

The first charge against Gov. Walker represents that he has labored to induce a Missourian by the name of HERNDON to vote at Kickapoo. When we heard the report we pronounced it false, because we felt it was in violation of his instructions from the President, and diametrically opposite to all his pledges made repeatedly to the Free State party and the public generally, and his expression to us *personally*. While at Lecompton the other day we chanced to meet Lieut. CARR of the U. S. Army, a gentleman from New York of unimpeachable integrity, and a personal acquaintance of ours. Lieut. Carr, we believe, is the aid of the Governor, and has generally accompanied his Excellency on his tours through the Territory. The Lieutenant states that he was with Gov. W. at Kickapoo, and that he was present at the interview with the Governor and Mr. Herndon. Gov. W. inquired of Mr. H. if he had voted. The latter replied that he had not; that he was a resident of Missouri. "Then, said the Governor, "you have no right to vote." This expression is in keeping with Gov. W's action and advice in regard to foreign interference in our elections, and agrees with his late address over his own signature, and to the fact that in carrying out the spirit of the address he had placed troops at the instance of the Free State party, at five points in Kansas, contiguous to the Missouri line, to prevent frauds upon the citizens, and particularly against voting by Missourians. It will be seen, then, that the above story is wholly false, and if reported was gotten up for effect.

Let us state here, that we were informed weeks ago by pro-slavery men, and by persons from Leavenworth and other places along the border, that immediately after the October election a concerted movement would be made by the pro-slavery party to get rid of Gov. Walker. This information we have communicated repeatedly to friends, and to the Governor himself. Of course we had no knowledge of the mode of attack; but we felt confident it would be made. We firmly believe that if Mr. Herndon, or any other men, are making such gross representations against Gov. W. they are doing it for effect; that it is a part of the great plan for getting his Excellency out of the way; and that they are laboring to make cats' paws of the Free State party in their dirty work; and from present appearances are likely to be quite successful. The pro-slavery party in the past has not hesitated to resort to fraud and falsehood, and even *perjury* to carry out their ends. The tendency of their late gross frauds has not been to give them a better character. We would earnestly caution the public that they be not too hasty in condemning the Governor on flying rumors, and newspaper reports; nor even volunteered and extra-judicial affidavits; for good men *have* been lied down, and others may be. There is danger of striking down our best friends when we allow such instrumentalities to be employed successfully in crushing them.

It is stated that a large number of U. S. troops voted under Gov. Walker's directions at Kickapoo, and the Leavenworth *Times* devotes a column and a half to that subject. Let us state the facts as we understand them:

When Gov. Walker wrote his late address to the people of Kansas, it has been contended, first, that no person could vote at the recent elections without having paid a tax. The pro-slavery Grand Jury of Lecompton some two months ago, had so decided in their letter to Judge Cato; he concurred most fully in that opinion. Attorney General WIER coincided in an elaborate argument. Under this formidable weight of authority Gov. W. addressed the Government at Washington stating most emphatically his opinion that the people could vote without the payment of this tax, and his determination to act on that opinion, with the view, however, to give additional force to his own views he requested those of the President and Cabinet. Now it is manifest that if the authorities had not concurred with Gov. W. in his views, they must have recalled him, and, therefore, he put his office and position at stake on this question, for the benefit of the people of Kansas; but most fortunately the question was so strongly and clearly argued by the Governor that the President and *all* his Cabinet—as he tells us in his late address—endorsed his opinion;

and if the peace of Kansas has been preserved, and the PEOPLE have elected their Delegate to Congress, and their Territorial Legislature, and shall for the first time obtain control of their own affairs we owe it most distinctly to this very just act on the part of the Governor. Now that the Governor should set about to destroy the work of his own hands seems incredible. What is the evidence to the contrary? It is said that the Governor interfered so far as to direct the troops, as stated above, to vote at Kickapoo against the Free State party. We would here ask, inasmuch as Gov. W. had 2,600 troops under his command, why he did not induce them *all* to vote, instead of the 40, as alleged at Kickapoo only? Now we believe the facts will turn out to be substantially as follows: When Gov. W. was preparing his address as to the qualification of voters, the first question which naturally presented itself to his consideration was this: As the organic act permits the Territorial Legislature of Kansas to prescribe the qualification of voters at every election but the first, does the proviso or the organic act, prohibit soldiers and persons attached to the army "*by reason of their being on service therein*" from voting at the first, or all subsequent elections? This question was decided in our favor, as his address fully shows. Now the Territorial enactment of Feb. 20, '57, declares that "*all* citizens of the United States, who have resided in the Territory six months before the election, shall be permitted to vote." The question: how was this organic law to be reconciled with the Territorial act on this point? We understand they were reconciled thus: that soldiers and persons attached to the army could *not vote* "by reason of their being on service therein," but if they possessed all the qualification of voters *independent* of such service, and were citizens of the United States, and had a *bona fide* residence of six months next preceding the election in the Territory, they had a right to vote under the Territorial law. That is, if a soldier, teamster, or mechanic, resided with his family in Missouri, he should not vote by reason of his being on service here, but if such soldier, teamster or mechanic, was a *bona fide* resident here, *independent* of such service, especially if prior to his enlistment, and had no other residence but this for the six months next preceding the election, he had a right to vote, not as a soldier, but as a *resident citizen.*

These, too, were Gov. Reeder's views, as we chance to know under the same organic law, as several officers at Fort Riley were permitted to vote as early as 1855, under the same constitution; and this right has never been previously questioned. Gov. W., however, as we understand, did not wish the soldiers to vote; indeed, we are told when this question was discussed at Fort Leavenworth for several days preceding the election, Gov. W. expressed a hope that the soldiers would not vote, though he gave no order on the subject, and had no right to give any. Now, how did any of them come to vote? We may state, the election having passed off quietly at Leavenworth on the first day, and going off with equal quietness on the second, the Governor, as we understand from Lieut. Carr, sometime after dinner on the second day rode to Kickapoo, not to participate in any barbacue, for none was given there, nor to take any part in the election, nor to interfere in any way in the proceedings, but to see that everything was passing off quietly there, and then to return to the Fort. Shortly after arriving at Kickapoo, as we have the statement from Lieut. Carr, the Governor was informed that several soldiers who had obtained leave of absence from the camp had voted, and they had actually voted the Free State ticket. Gov. Walker was then urged by citizens to withdraw the expression of his wishes in order that the other soldiers, if they desired, might also participate in the election. After considerable delay and hesitation, he did consent, provided those soldiers only should vote, who, independent of their being in the service, had the citizenship and evidence required by law. And a few of them, our Free State friends say, to the number of forty, did vote; but how they voted or for whom, Gov. W. declares, as Lieut. Carr states, he never knew, and does not now know how they voted, as the Governor rode away immediately to the Fort, and the election was then drawing to a close; but even if they all voted the pro-slavery ticket, which is absolutely denied, it would not change the result, either for Delegate to Congress, or Territorial Legislature, or any county officer.

Lieut. Carr also states that none of the officers went to the polls, and that they did not even intimate to the men which way their own political proclivities lay, but only gave permission to go to the polls to such men as desired it, and their opinion is that not more than twenty-five did go.

But how as to Johnson county, which does change the result as regards the Territorial Legislature? Why, Gov. Walker, at the request of the Free State party, sent a strong force consisting of a battery and three companies of artillery, equal to a force of 1,300 men, under the command of Col. Brooks, formerly of Massachusetts, himself a Free State man, to Shawnee in Johnson county, the supposed point of danger, to prevent illegal voting, especially from Missouri. Westport in Missouri, but three miles distant from the Shawnee precinct, was the anticipated point for the concentration of the Missourians, and from this point originally, they intended to come. This was evident from previous experience, as well as from what occurred before and after the election. Col. Brooks arrived at Shawnee the day before the election. When Col. B. arrived, he states, that he was called upon by the celebrated *Col. Titus* and also by a Mr. *Anderson* of Westport, who complained bitterly of the stationing of troops there, and said that "The people would be compelled to vote at the point of the bayonet."

Col. B., however, remained firm at his post, exhibiting Gov. W's address against foreign voters as his letter of instructions. What followed? Why the Missourians changed their place of voting and went on the second day to Oxford, which is twelve miles distant from Shawnee, and some fifteen miles from Westport, a point directly on the border of Missouri opposite the town of Little Santa Fe. Here the fraud was perpetrated, not on the first, but quietly on the second day of the election. Indeed we do not believe any of these votes were given, but were merely entered and counted as such, as appears by the certificates on file at Lecompton, to the number of 1,538 on this second day, which was impossible, or even one-half that number, to be polled on one day. Now it is upon the Oxford precinct of Johnson county that a majority of the voters for the Territorial Delegate to Congress, probably, and certainly a majority of the Delegates to the Territorial Legislature will turn. If this Oxford precinct is rejected, the people will have the Delegate and the Territorial Legislature, and the result will mainly depend upon the action of Gov. Walker. If he is true to the solemn pledges contained in his inaugural address, in his Topeka speeches, and his late proclamation on the tax question, he will reject this fraudulent return with scorn and indignation. This we firmly believe he will do from his past course. Indeed if he did not wish the people to rule Kansas why did he issue his address on the tax question, which address, if we do succeed, issued under the most trying circumstances, will have given us peace and victory?

We are happy to learn that a protest has been signed and forwarded to the Governor and Secretary in regard to these Oxford returns, which will be found in another column. If the Governor proves false to his pledges, and not till then, will be the time to seek other modes of redress.

If the last resort of freemen shall become necessary, let us at least first know whether Governor Walker will not do his whole duty, and render the last alternative unnecessary.

Let us have our rights, "*peaceably* if we can, *forcibly* if we must."

And thus my sale to Gov. Walker, of which some very small men have accused me, and have continued to repeat almost down to the period this book was put to press, my consideration, as the facts show, the freedom of Kansas, and, incidental thereto, the freedom of the civilized world from chattel slavery, was cotingent on this action. My compeers were similarly maligned. Would that our traducers, who judged of our market value by their own worthlessness, had realized a millionth fraction of that consideration for their malicious libels.

CHAPTER XV.

Score One for Freedom!

LEAVING the Executive office, I sought the hotel, where I found Mr. Wier waiting with deep anxiety my return. I had not seen or communicated with him since going to Gov. Walker's room, soon after three o'clock, and my long absence probably recalled former incidents in Kansas history, when committees, representing the people, sent to Lecompton to consult Territorial officials, were arrested for some fictitious offense and imprisoned.

We set out for Lawrence, and made a speedy trip home. Col. Eldridge and two other gentlemen, names not remembered, called at my office, to whom I gave a brief account of the interview with the Governor, and read the editorials in manuscript, written under his dictation. I also stated the promise he made me, to reject the fraudulent returns; and that on the following Monday he, with Secretary Stanton, would drive down to the newly-found city of Oxford, with its dense voting population, and on his return they would make public their decision.

This intelligence quickly spread over Lawrence, and the excitement was greatly allayed thereby. On Saturday the editorial referred to appeared in the Herald of Freedom, and on the Monday following Gov. Walker, Secretary Stanton, and, I think, Lieut. Carr, with the government ambulance, passed down

from Lecompton, on their way to Oxford, stopping
for a short time at the Herald of Freedom office,
where they made much mirth over the newly-discov-
ered city, whose name was unknown to all of us until
these returns gave it notoriety.

At Fish's, a place of entertainment, a little distance
below Blue Jacket's, they met a small party, of which
G. W. Deitzler was one, from Lawrence, who had
been down to the State line to learn facts, and were
on their return. A much larger party were on their
way to arrest the Judges, if they could be found, and
these passed the Governor's party at this place.

John Speer is reported as intimating, at Bismarck
Grove, on the occasion of the Quarter Century cele-
bration, in September, 1879, that the threats of these
men induced Gov. Walker and Secretary Stanton to
reject those fraudulent returns. The writer had the
Governor's promise, several days before, as narrated
in the preceding chapter, to so act; and this knowledge was in possession of five persons *certain,* and
such others as could be trusted with the secret. We
regret that Mr. Speer was not of this number, then
he would have done the Governor better justice.

The Governor and Secretary were absent some two
or three days, when they returned to Lawrence,
unrolled in the hall of the Morrow House, and exhib-
ited to the public the Oxford returns, measuring
nearly fifty feet in length, with the names of 1,626
persons, who it was claimed voted at that precinct,
and which seemed to have been copied from some
city directory. They stated that the city, with so
large a population, contained just six houses; that the
village of Santa Fe, Mo., containing twenty houses,

was separated from it by a street, the center of which was the State and Territorial line; that the people of all classes ridiculed the idea of there being one-tenth the number of the people represented as voting in the place during the two days of the election. They returned to Lecompton on the 19th, published a proclamation rejecting the returns, and issued certificates of election to the Free State candidates.

While the Free State residents of the Territory were greatly rejoiced at the result, the excitement, which had been so violent at Lawrence and other Free State towns, was now transferred to the proslavery residents of the Territory, being most bitter at Lecompton, where the principal leaders of the party resided. Threats of violence to the Governor and Secretary were heard on every hand.

The principal residents of Lawrence, to the number of over a hundred, joined in a letter, addressed to the Executive and Secretary, thanking them for their just action, and inviting them to remove to Lawrence, promising them full protection against the "fiends who desired to crush them, and trample on the dearest rights of the people." The writer, accompanied by Robert Morrow, conveyed the letter to the Governor, who we found quite ill, with a high fever, at the residence of Secretary Stanton, some two miles east of Lecompton. The labor and excitement of the last few weeks had been too much for the Governor's age and feeble constitution.

But a little time after our arrival, Secretary Stanton entered the room, and introduced a Mr. Faunt. The latter gave the Governor a sort of process, designed for a mandamus, issued by Judge Cato, dated Oct. 20th, directed to Robert J. Walker and Frederick P. Stanton, "enjoining" them to issue certificates of election to the pro-slavery candidates therein named.

The Governor sprang from bed greatly excited, and declared that Judge Cato had forgotten his position; that he was subordinate to the Executive, instead of the Executive to himself; that he was so ignorant of law he had issued what was evidently designed for a *peremptory* mandamus, directed to them instead of to the Marshal of the Territory— the ministerial officer of the court; that if issued at all it should have been *alternative,* leaving it with them to do as commanded, or show cause for not doing so. Secretary Stanton, who was also a lawyer by profession, was as denunciatory as the Governor of Judge Cato's action, who was attempting to deprive them of the prerogative of counting the returns, which the law exclusively vested in them. They said the Legislative Assembly could only review their action, as regarded its own members, and Congress as regarded the delegate to that body. Instead of making a point with these officials, the latter were still farther estranged. Indeed, the breach was made so broad by this action it was never healed.

On the 21st the Governor and Secretary joined in a letter to the people of Lawrence, thanking them for their kind invitation to remove to that city. They said the interests of the Territory required their presence at the capital, and "no hazard of personal consequences would deter" them from remaining there and faithfully discharging their duties. They also declared in that letter: "From our first inspec-

tion of the Oxford returns we never hesitated as to
their rejection," and announced that they had rejected
as spurious and illegal the returns both from Oxford
and McGee county.

The answer of the officials to the mandamus of
Judge Cato was decidedly interesting. They showed
conclusively, that the Judge had no jurisdiction in
the premises; that such authority had never been
exercised in any State or Territory, and quoted numerous decisions of the Supreme Court of the United
States adverse to such jurisdiction; that the rights of
the opposition candidates would be affected, and that
they should be made a party; that they had issued
certificates of election to the adverse claimants,
before process was served on them, and that such certificates were in the hands of the officers and beyond
recall; that if, in disregard of all this, the Judge
decided adversely, they begged an appeal to the
Supreme Court; and if they were still held in con-
tempt, and the Court ordered their imprisonment,
and feared the interference of the populace, they
would issue an order to the military to place such
force as his honor should deem necessary at the service of the Marshal, to enable him to hold them safely
in custody.

The laugh was on the Judge, and his ruling, whatever it may have been, was never made public.

The reader inquires: "Was it really the intention
of Gov. Walker to go back on his pledges?" This
was at the time, and has been ever since a subject of
earnest consideration. The opinion arrived at then,
and which the writer has seen no occasion to change,
was, that he was angered by the course of the radical

press, particularly the Lawrence *Republican* and the Leavenworth *Times*, the latter a semi-conservative paper, which contained a lengthy article filled with personal abuse and misrepresentation of the Governor, which he had just seen. He no doubt felt that if his best acts were to be falsified, and that continually, he would retort in a way which would be effective. During the entire day before my interview he had been closeted with the most prominent pro-slavery leaders. Gov. Walker had lost his political standing in Mississippi, overborne by the disunion-Jefferson-Davis school, and of course hoped to regain it in Kansas. Probably he had been encouraged by promises of favor and position under the Lecompton Constitution. Be this as it may, the Governor's whole manner and language showed conclusively to my mind, that his purpose was to count the pro-slavery men into office and the Free State men out. When assured of continued confidence and support from the Herald of Freedom, and possibly his personal fears were aroused, he resolved to stem the tide of opposition in his own party, act with the stronger and do justice to them. *

Secretary Stanton, on the contrary, had not shared so liberally in the personal abuse of the radical press and the letter-writers. He had removed to Kansas with his family, and determined to make the Territory his permanent home. His interests and future were of a different character from those of the Governor. A younger man, with more personal courage, he had resolved from the first to do right. Dining at

*See Secretary Stanton's letter in the Appendix.

my own table, a few weeks before, he said, in so many
words, written down within an hour from their utterance: "My right hand shall sooner be severed from
my body than I will sign a certificate of election
where I am satisfied a person is elected by fraud." I
thought at the time, and wrote soon after [See Herald of Freedom, of Oct. 24, 1857, 2d page, 3d column,] "Let Secretary Stanton keep that solemn
pledge, and his name will be endeared to the people
of Kansas." He kept it faithfully, and I now write
with pleasure, he and Gov. Walker, in this emergency,
were the people's REAL DELIVERERS!

Thus the first step in the Herald of Freedom platform, of July 4th, was successfully taken, and so far
as a voice in Congress thereafter was concerned, we
were victorious, as also with regard to the Territorial
Legislature, and the local administration of the laws;
but all the while we had been thus actively endeavor-
ing to regain our rights in these directions, we were
conscious a new danger was threatening, which was
still more formidable than those we had so successfully encountered.

CHAPTER XVI.

IN TRACING the action of the Free State party to get possession of the Territorial government, we have neglected to watch the State movement, under the proposed Lecompton Constitution. It was evident the pro-slavery leaders had an understanding with President Buchanan and his Cabinet, and that all their movements were inspired at, and directed from Washington. Even Gov. Walker was instructed to recognize the Convention as a legal one, and give it his protection.

When the Constitutional Convention assembled at Lecompton, on the 7th of September, 1857, the troops were still before Lawrence. On the 9th of September Col. Cooke received imperative orders from Washington, to remove his command, without delay, to Fort Leavenworth. Gov. Walker was greatly incensed because of this, and declared he would not remain in the Territory without the troops to aid in maintaining order. He left immediately on the receipt of the dispatch for the Fort, hoping to get the order countermanded. He failed. On the morning of the 11th the entire regiment was on the move, and the beleagured city was relieved of its long surveillance.

With the removal of the troops, as if fearful of its personal security, the Convention adjourned until the

19th of October, late enough, before again assembling, to learn the result of the Territorial election to be held on the 5th.

In our "Reminiscences of old John Brown," published in 1880, mentioning the period from the 7th of August, to the 2d of November, 1857, and the resting of Capt. Brown at Tabor, Iowa, with the leading spirits of his command; his brief visit to Lawrence, change of plans, and then to the East, we said, page 52, second column:

"I have one of the most exciting chapters in Kansas history, to detail *sometime*, which occurred during this interesting period, and which may partially explain John Brown's reasons for hovering on the borders of Kansas during this interval. To introduce it in these pages would require the introduction of other characters, which are not at present subjects of inquiry, hence it is reserved for another occasion."

That occasion is before us, and we hasten to its narration:

It is remembered that on the 16th of July, Gen. Lane was instructed to organize the military forces in Kansas "for the protection of the ballot box.' But this was not the *source* of his authority. A secret Order was instituted by Lane, ostensibly to oppose the aggressions of the slave power in Kansas. This organization was under the management of those who opposed the voting policy. They were always *talking* about fighting the government if it stood in their way. Their leaders fled the Territory on the first approach of danger, to return when all was over, and renew the agitation which cooler heads had allayed during their absence.

Wm. A. Phillips, the special Kansas correspondent

of the New York *Tribune*, wrote his journal, dated June 17, 1857: "Mark my words! Nothing but a sufficient force of the United States army will be able to keep that Constitutional Convention in Kansas."

At Osawkee, in July, while the Delaware Trust Lands were being sold, speaking of his military organization, Gen. Lane said: "They will assemble at Lecompton on the day the Constitutional Convention assembles for review."

I think it was near noon of Saturday, the 17th of October, 1857, Augustus Wattles, at that time our associate editor, entered the sanctum of the Herald of Freedom office in an excited manner, very unusual to him, and said hurriedly:

"Why, Brown, we are on the eve of a revolution! Gen. Lane has ordered the organized Free State forces of the Territory to assemble on Monday next, with arms and three days' supply of provisions, the purpose of which is to march on Lecompton and kill every member of the Constitutional Convention. It is also his purpose to wipe out the Territorial Government, and set up the Topeka Government. The United States troops are *en route* for Utah, and now is thought a good time to strike. Unless headed off in his insane movement, notwithstanding our recent success at the polls, all is lost; for the country will never indorse this scheme of wholesale murder!"

I questioned him sufficiently to know he was making a statement on positive knowledge. Catching my hat I rushed to the different business houses, and made them acquainted with the information Mr. Wattles had imparted. G. W. Collamore, G. W. Smith, Wesley and Charles Duncan (both now living at Lawrence,) George Ford, Columbus Hornsby, and, indeed, all the substantial men whom I met, were invited to assemble immediately in a vacant room over the store of Messrs. Duncan, for consultation. In a very short time they were in session, probably from fifty to one hundred. We organized with Judge Smith as chairman. The object of the meeting was briefly stated, when, on motion of Mr. Collamore, a committee of three was appointed to invite Gen. Lane to attend the meeting.

The committee soon returned accompanied by the General. The chairman stated to him what the people had casually learned, in regard to his proposed descent on Lecompton, and the assassination of the members of the Constitutional Convention, and inquired of him if they were correctly informed.

The General at first seemed to evade a direct answer. He entered into a disquisition on the wrongs the people of Kansas had sustained from the pro-slavery party, and was really eloquent, *in his way*, as he recounted our grievances. While he was speaking in this strain, avoiding an answer to Judge Smith's interrogatory, a crowd of young men, "boys," as Lane always called them, came pouring in at the lower end of the room, and, as was their habit, when Lane pointed his long, bony finger and said, "Great God!" in his peculiar way, they cheered heartily. Seeing that his backers were with him, he became more bold and defiant. I was without writing material, but with pencil, old envelopes, backs of letters and on finger nails, wrote down the substance of Lane's wildest utterances.

The speaker, having observed what I was doing, stopped in the midst of his extravagant expressions and said:

"George, do me the personal favor not to report this speech."

Of course I gratified him, and ceased taking further written notes; but carefully treasured in memory the substance of what he said, which is still retained as if repeated yesterday.

It was apparent, by the vociferous cheering, long before he concluded, that then and there was not the time or place to vote on the question, so an adjournment was had until evening, in front of the Morrow House.

During the afternoon the whole town was advised of the character of the proposed evening meeting, and the attendance was very large. Judge Smith called the meeting to order. Gen. Lane desired a further hearing, and was given the temporary stand. He came prepared for the occasion, and his backers were with him. They cheered him to the echo. Mr. Collamore and myself moved among the crowd, and both despaired of the result.

Some other person, I think it was Judge Schuyler, followed Lane, who, in a mild and pacificatory speech, deprecated such a condition of the country, and expressed his opinion that the occasion did not demand such extreme measures as were proposed.

As the second speaker retired, Joel K. Goodin mounted the rostrum. Mr. Collamore and myself expressed surprise to see him take the stand. He commenced by saying he had received an order from his superior officer to report at Lawrence, armed and

equipped for efficient military duty, and to bring provisions and camp-equipage for three days' service;
that, "in obedience to that order, I am here to-night
with my command, having made the journey all the
way from Centropolis especially to obey it. [Cheers.]
I feel that the occasion is one which demands great
sacrifices. [Cheers.] We have worked all summer in
a quiet way to regain the rights wrested from us by
the invasion of the 30th of March, '55, and in spite of
fraud and artifice we have triumphed. We have seen
this Territory torn and disturbed by hostile parties;
men murdered in cold blood; our homes burned, and
our families scattered, and we, at times compelled to
seek personal safety in flight. Gov. Geary came here
and restored order, and Gov. Walker has bent all his
energies in the same direction. Under his wise
administration, we saw in imagination a brilliant
future before us. But here is that Lecompton Constitutional Convention threatening us with new danger, when we supposed our dangers were all passed.
Gen. Lane tells us that further peaceful measures are
out of the question; that our only remedy for this
new trouble is by shedding blood. I fully agree with
him! [Boisterous cheers.] Nothing but blood will
quiet this agitation, and restore tranquility to Kansas.
Nothing but blood will make Kansas a Free State.
[Cheers.] I came here expressly to spill blood, and
I propose to do it before I return home. [Protracted
cheering.] It is not just that the whole country
shall be convulsed; that disorder and violence shall
be continued; that the perpetuity of the government
shall be endangered by a revolution, when a little
waste of worthless blood will restore order and

tranquility again. [Cheers on cheers.] But I may
differ with some of you as to the proper place to
begin this blood-spilling business. [Hear! hear!] No
person has occasioned more strife, or been the more
fruitful cause of our disturbances than—James H.
Lane! He demands blood! We all want it; but it is
his blood that is demanded at this time; and *if he
presses on his assassination project, I propose he
shall be the first person to contribute in that direction.*" [The wildest cheering possible, greatly prolonged, followed.]*

*Joel K. Goodin, Esq., after reading Chapter 16, in which he
plays an important part, wrote:

OTTAWA, Kan., March 30, 1881.

MY OLD FRIEND:—I received yesterday the galley proof of
your "Blood and Thunder" article, [Chap. 16,] in your "Reminiscences of Gov. Walker," and have carefully read it. It freshly
brought to mind many past scenes and incidents. My little
"blood speech" is correctly reported so near as I can remember it
—at least you have given its import. We were being called from
our homes every few days to satisfy the ambition and caprice of
the uneasy and tireless Lane, and were becoming not only disgusted but mad, and proposed to have it "dried up.' A most
fearful and wanton system of savagery and assassination was being
planned by Lane, which the Free State party were intended to be
held responsible for, not only to our own government, but to the
world. For one I was unwilling to take any such responsibility.
Those I had with me felt the same way, and urged that I give
public expression to their views. This I did fearlessly and plainly,
and was most happy then, as I am now, that I contributed something towards turning the tide of proposed outlawry and bloodshed
into the channels of peace.

In the early days we always had a bad element at Lawrence. I
refer to the young, undisciplined bloods, who were without repu-
table means of support, always ready and anxious to take part in
any hellish scheme set on foot to stir up strife. This element was
largely controlled, or, rather, was ready to effervesce at the *dic-*

Gen. Lane seemed perfectly confounded. The whole throng were taken by surprise; and the business portion of it were delighted beyond expression, that some person had the ability and sufficient force of character to meet a bold, bad man, and throttle his murderous plans at their inception. The writer thought it a good time for action. Hurrying to the stand, he said:

"It is evident from the statements of Gen. Lane, and what we have heard from others, that there will be a goodly number of people in Lawrence by Monday next, who feel as we do, that the convention about re-assembling in Lecompton is not a body representing the people of Kansas; that I propose we go there on Monday next, in a quiet and orderly manner, as peaceable citizens, avoiding all riotous demonstrations, to arrive by noon, if possible, and there, before the hall in which that body is assembled, formally protest against that convention framing a Constitution for us; that they are a body foreign to our

tum of Lane. *Their* time was nothing; while we in the country had to undergo many severe privations in running after Lane's orders, messages and commands as self-imposed military dictator. No wonder we tired and felt in a degree revengeful. For years I could not agree with him, and was constantly in his way in the "Executive Committee," thwarting his ridiculously impracticable, reckless, extravagant and sometimes atrocious plans and suggestions. Usually I had Judge Smith, yourself, and Holliday, when present, with me, which gave us the majority. He would come and fume, but we were firm and inflexible, so he would soon drop his crazy project, to immediately concoct another equally objectionable. I feel that we did our duty well, and am content to abide the decision of the future historian who shall review our actions. Truly Yours, J. K. GOODIN.

soil, with no interests in common with the people of Kansas."

Gen. Lane stepped forward, seconded the proposition, and made a short speech in its favor. A committee was appointed to make arrangements, appoint marshals to lead the procession, and to do everything necessary to carry successfully into execution the measure.

On Monday the procession was formed, and proceeded quietly to Lecompton, where they formally organized, with P. C. Schuyler as President. A committee on resolutions was appointed, of which Wm. Hutchinson was chairman. While the committee were in consultation on the resolutions, Gen. L made one of his most effective political speeches.

The protesting resolutions were reported, and adopted by acclamation. Maclean, of the Land Office, Stewart, of the Convention, and Sam Young, a prominent lawyer, all pro-slavery, made speeches; to which Gen. Lane replied; after which the protestants adjourned, and retraced their steps to Lawrence. All felt that the movement set on foot to drench the country in blood had been fortunately turned into an instrumentality of good.

In this connection, I recall an interview with Gov. Robinson, in which this abortive attempt of Gen. Lane to inaugurate a revolution was under discussion. He mentioned being present at a meeting of Lane's *secret* military organization, in Masonic Hall, the date of which he did not remember, at which he was initiated a member, At the conclusion of the ceremony Gen. Lane, in his characteristic style

recounted the work before the Order. He said: "I
have ordered Gen. —— to strike at Leavenworth;
Gen. —— to strike at Atchison; Gen. —— to strike
at Doniphan; Gen. —— to strike at Kickapoo; now
it remains for you to say what shall be done with
Lecompton;" his extreme modesty, no doubt, preventing him from assuming command of the expedition against that delectable town, preferrimg the
Order, of which he was the head, to so depute him.
Gov. Robinson said, that after a period of silence he
was called upon for remarks. Rising and addressing
the chair, he inquired by what authority this proce-
dure, to attack and destroy pro-slavery towns, had
been inaugurated? Gen. Lane replied: "By direction of the Military Board." The Governor continued: "The Board can give no such authority. It
would be foreign to the purpose of its organization."
He then gave notice that he should oppose any such
movement with all the ability he possessed. Gov.
Robinson never met with the secret conclave again,
possibly feeling like the intruding guest ejected from
a hotel. Finding himself forcibly thrust into the
street, slowly rising, surveying his condition, and
brushing the dust from his person, an observer ven-
tured the question, "How did you feel as you were
tumbling down stairs?" "Very much as if I was not
wanted there!" was the prompt reply. It is very certain Gov. Robinson never desired to enter that mystic
circle again; and his readiness to suppress an incipient revolution, set on foot by the "Grim Chieftain"
and his Danite band, did not tend to make him more
popular with that class of men.
    Whether this proposed general movement against

the leading pro-slavery towns of the Territory, was
planned to come off at the same time with the proposed military descent on Lecompton, we are not
advised; but, from the date of an order in Gen. Lane's
handwriting, signed by him, and now in our possession, directed to "Capt. Charley Lenhart," ordering
him to "take such number of active young men as you
shall deem necessary, and proceed with as little delay
as possible to colonize Kickapoo," we are convinced
that the two periods were concurrent in time.

So, too, in this proposed assasination of all the members of this Constitutional Convention, we have the
secret of old John Brown remaining so long at rest—
from the 7th of August to the 2d of November—with
all the members of his clan, who were members of this
secret organization, and familiar with its plans, hovering on the Kansas border, watching hourly for
advices from Kansas, delaying for twelve days after
the period fixed for striking the fatal blow; thence,
with a single son, overland to Lawrence; a brief interview with Gen. E. B. Whitman, a high functionary
and second in command in this secret organization; a
short visit to Gov. Robinson, who frankly told him he
was damaging the cause of Free Kansas by his pred-
atory operations along the border, and then his return
east, *"disgusted with the Kansas leaders!"*

CHAPTER XVII.

In a New Role.

FROM the first settlement down to the period of which I write, the whole Democratic press, North and South, seemed united against the Free State pioneers of Kansas, and the cause they represented. The administration at Washington was Democratic. As it had joined hands with the usurpers, of course the Democratic press sustained them; and the reader of those journals floated along with the popular current.

Cogitating on this condition of things, with a large Democratic exchange list, I saw that the St. Louis *Republican* was the text book which furnished the key-note for the party, from the President down to the meanest Border Ruffian who made his annual visit to Kansas to do its voting.

Henry Clay Pate, of Westport, Mo., was the Kansas correspondent of the *Republican,* and his criminally-false statements were continually going the rounds of his party papers, always to the prejudice of the cause for which we were laboring.

Recalling these facts, it occurred to me that if the tone of that paper could be changed, a great good could be accomplished. I wrote out at length the leading incidents in the preceding chapter, added to it some facts in my possession regarding the movements of Gov. Walker and Sec'y Stanton, was careful that every statement should bear the severest criticism, and sent the same to the *Republican*, placing it at the editor's disposal, stating, in an accompanying letter, that if he wanted a correspondent who was intimately acquainted with every fact in Kansas history from its first settlement; who held confidential relations with both the Territorial officials and the Free State party; and who would pledge himself *never to write a falsehood*, then it would give me pleasure to fill that position.

By return mail, I received a letter from the proprietor of the *Republican*, stating that my proposition was accepted; that the letter received would appear in the next morning's paper; that he wanted me to write at least one letter a week, and as much oftener, even if it was daily, as I had important events to communicate; that he would pay me five dollars for each letter used, and would place no restrictions on me, only to keep my promise to write the truth let it militate against whom it might. It further stated that Mr. Pate was already discharged, and they had no other correspondent from thenceforth but myself. I made a similar arrangement to write for the N. Y. *Commercial Advertiser*, and a few letters to the N. Y. *Evening Post*.

I communicated to no one, not even my nearest friends, the position I was filling; and to avoid suspicion of the postmaster, the letters were directed to the editors by name, and not to the papers. I had the pleasure of seeing those letters copied into the almost entire Democratic press of the North, headed with heavy display lines of "The Truth from Kansas

at Last," "Wholesale Assassination Proposed by Jim
Lane," "Gov. Walker Playing an Honest Hand,"
"The Free State Party Largely in the Majority,"
"The Lecompton Constitution Repudiated by the
People," and thus on through successive numbers of
the paper.

Not only the Democratic press, but Republican
journals as well, copied these letters, usually with
approving comments, at the same time calling attention to the changed tone of the opposition.

Congress was about to convene. As I was conscious
the fraudulent Constitution would be submitted to
that body at an early day in its session, and recognizing that Senator Douglas was a power in the Senate Chamber, I wrote that distinguished gentleman a
long letter, showed up the iniquity of the Constitutional Convention, and, to secure his confidence and
assure him that I was "behind the scenes," I sent him
a ritual of a secret Order, printed at the Herald of
Freedom office. The Order was instituted at an
early day, had ceased to be operative and had been
superseded by another. Of the latter facts I said
nothing. Mr. Douglas wrote me a very pleasant let-
tor in reply; thanked me for having communicated
such important information, which he would make
use of when he had occasion to again address the
Senate on Kansas affairs. At the same time he made
numerous inquiries in regard to various matters
touching that Constitution; of the body by which it
was made; their election, etc. Any one having the
curiosity to know what Mr. Douglas said of the writer,
without mentioning his name, or of his action to

defeat that Constitution, can consult the Congressional files of that time. Sufficient for me to say, from henceforth Mr. Douglas opposed that villainous Constitution, and the ruffians who called it into being, with all the energy of which he was so largely the master.

Those who are willing to do the opposition justice were frank to concede had Mr. Douglas' great influence been turned in the other channel, notwithstanding all our struggles to the contrary, in all probability we should have been admitted into the Union a slave State. I am glad to record in this connection, that other gentlemen exercised great influence with Senator Douglas at this critical period in our history. Gov. Robinson held a long personal interview with him, soon after the bogus Constitution reached Washington; and Gov. Walker relied upon Douglas' efforts in the Senate to secure justice to Kansas, since it was denied by President Buchanan and his infamous Cabinet.

I shall have occasion in our next chapter, to show stil further valuable services my position as correspondent of the St. Louis *Republican* enabled me to perform in antagonizing the Constitution.

CHAPTER XVIII.

New Dangers to be Combatted.

THE CONSTITUTIONAL Convention re-convened on the 19th of October, without a quorum, however, for several days, as the publicity given to Lane's assassination scheme frightened the more timorous of that body into temporary exile from the capital. Gov. Walker succeeded in getting a small force from Fort Leavenworth, under the immediate command of Maj. Sedgwick, to protect the Convention from the violence of the people for whom they were making a Constitution, after which they resumed their work of forging chains for those they wished to enslave.

That body completed its labors on the 7th of November, and made provision for submitting only the article relating to slavery to the people. They had taken the precaution to provide for the existence of slavery by other articles of the Constitution; so that in reality it made no difference in the legal effect whether the article referred to was adopted or rejected; slavery was still, by its provisions, the fundamental law of the State, and was placed beyond the power of repeal.

Both Gov. Walker and Secretary Stanton had labored with the members of the Convention to procure the submission of the Constitution as a whole to the people, but in this they were defeated.

Soon after the adjournment of the Convention

Gov. Walker, under the pretext of important personal business, left for Washington, he said, to be absent three or four weeks. Arriving there he held long personal and very animated interviews with President Buchanan, trying to induce him to give the Constitution no countenance; but all to no purpose. Finally, on the 17th of December, the Governor wrote a long letter to Secretary Cass, reviewing the condition of Kansas affairs, denouncing the attempt to rob the people of their liberties, and tendered his resignation, which was formally accepted on the following day.

There seemed no other way to get a legal expression of the popular will with regard to the Constitution, to go before Congress, than through action of the Legislature.* That body, under existing law, would not meet in regular session until the 4th of January, 1858, the very day provided in the Constitution for the election of officers under it.

*"The plan of an extra session of the Legislature, to meet the extraordinary crisis in our Territorial affairs, *was first publicly advocated by us* in a short speech to our fellow citizens, over Messrs. Duncan's store, on the 17th of October last, though we had previously suggested it to our associate, Mr. Wattles. Since then we have been unremitting in our exertions to get an extra session convened, and on Monday last, had a long interview with Acting Gov. Stanton on the subject, and drew up in our own hand the application, since signed by the members of the Legislative Assembly, as also the indorsement by the citizens which we led off in signing, asking him to convene that body."—Herald of Freedom, Dec. 5, 1857, first page, eighth column. See further in this direction, closing sentence of first article, third page, of Nov. 7; also second column and closing of first article on fourth column, Nov. 14; and second page, sixth column, of Dec. 19, article headed, "Stealing their Thunder." It is wonderful to see what claims are set up for others in this direction. See John Speer's speech published in the Kansas Memorial, p. 180.

While Gov. Walker was yet at Leavenworth, preparatory to descending the Missouri, he was waited upon by a committee from Lawrence, asking him to convene the newly elected Legislature. He declined, giving as a reason that he had already passed the responsibilities of the executive offce to Secretary Stanton, who, by virtue of the Organic Act, would be Acting Governor during his absence.

Acting Gov. Stanton was beseiged from all quarters for a like purpose. John Speer, in his *reported* speech at Bismarck Grove, September, 1879, represented that Col. Eldridge was instrumental in securing a promise, on certain conditions, for the issuance of the desired proclamation; and that he carried the petition of the members of the Legislature to the Governor asking his action in the premises. It is *merely possible some* of the statements made by Speer are correct; for each person having influence with Mr. Stanton, was doing his best to attain that end. The facts, however, will be best determined when each prominent actor shall report his own individual experience in that direction. As Gov. Stanton was yet living when these pages were first published, I took the more pleasure in stating what I knew about it, and appealed to him to correct me if I misrepresented in the slightest degree.*

*Secretary Stanton was born in Alexandria, D. C., December 22, 1814, and died in Ocala, Florida, June 4, 1894. He was a man of sterling ability, a lawyer by education, and for a time a Representative in Congress from Tennessee. He identified himself with the Free State party during its closing days, and, like Gov. Walker, was a faithful supporter of the Constitution and the Union, in opposition to the political heresies of Secession. A letter from him in the Appendix indorses such facts as are herein stated as came under his observation.

A petition was drawn up asking Gov. Stanton to convene the Legislature. It was professedly signed by a majority of the members of the Legislature, many of whose names, however, were signed to it by Lane, as the members were scattered over the Territory, and were difficult of access. That fact was well known to Gov. Stanton. The instrument, instead of being carried to the Governor by Col. Eldridge, was carried by Capt. Samuel Walker, who, by the way, was living in Lawrence, a distant relative of Gov. Walker, when these pages were originally published. After receiving it, Gov. Stanton called at my office, and we had a long conversation in regard to an extra session. I urged the necessity of it, and pressed the point with all the logic I could muster. He agreed with me as to the necessity of such a measure, and thought it the most effective weapon which could be employed in Congress to defeat that Constitution; to show by a legal vote of the people that nineteen-twentieths of them are opposed to it; but, he urged: "So soon as intelligence shall reach Washington of official action in that direction, my head will be lopped off, and I shall be deprived of further power to aid you."

I inquired of him what the effect would be if the Kansas correspondent of the St. Louis *Republican* would write a letter to that journal setting forth that the people were terribly convulsed because of their fears of being admitted into the Union under that Constitution; that unless something was done, and immediately, to allay the excitement, there was great probability it would break out in new scenes of violence and disorder, requiring a strong military force to suppress it; that the Acting Governor was well advised concerning this condition of things, and the pressure is so great and the danger so imminent it is probable he will feel compelled to grant the popular request, and issue the desired proclamation. He inquired:

"Are you acquainted with this correspondent?"

"I am."

"How soon can you see him?"

"Within a very short time."

"Do you think he will be able to write the letter proposed by two o'clock this afternoon?"

"I think so."

"Get him to write it and let me see it. I will go to dinner, and call here at two o'clock promptly. See if he can insure the forwarding of an advance slip from the *Republican* office to President Buchanan. This will be important."

Gov. Stanton left for dinner, and the letter for the *Republican* was written during his absence.

On his return at two o'clock, I read him the letter, which appeared a few days after in the St. Louis *Republican.*

"Have you any objection to communicating to me the name of this correspondent?"

"*Sub rosa,* Governor?"

"Yes, in strictest confidence, if required."

"It is granted you on that condition. I have had the honor of acting in that capacity for the last month or more."

"Well, I am astonished! Gov. Walker and I have talked this matter over several times, but we could not arrive at any satisfactory conclusion as to the author of those letters. He was as much unknown

to us as the author of the Junius letters. We agreed
it was some person in our confidence, as also in the
confidence of the leaders of the Free State party, and
somebody who was not afraid to tell the truth. We
guessed everybody but you. The fact that you had
not the aid of your associate for a long time, and your
editorial columns were so full, we supposed it would
be impossible for you to do any outside work."

The Governor thanked me for having done him
and Governor Walker full justice in all these letters;
that they had given them backbone as they were seen
floating through the press, with the almost entire
commendation of all parties.

"And you will forward this by first mail to the
Republican, and write the editor to send a corrected
proof-slip to the President. And will you embody
the substance of it in your forthcoming paper?"

"I will."

"Your paper is dated on Saturday?"

"Yes; but I go to press on Friday." I think this
was on Thursday.

"Do so, and I will come down on Tuesday next and
issue a proclamation, provided I can have satisfactory
assurance that the Legislature, when so convened,
will limit its action to merely submitting the Lecompton Constitution to a vote of all the people."

The article referred to appeared as a part of the
leader in the issue of the Herald of Freedom of Nov.
21, '57. In the concluding paragraph we said, in
italics: " *We have not a doubt but the Legislature
will be convened.*" In our issue of Dec. 5th, first
page, third column, we quoted the petition of the
members of the Legislature, including those "simu-

lated" by Lane, and also an agreement, drawn up by myself, and signed, "G. W. Brown, G. W. Smith, C. Robinson, J. H. Lane, and upwards of one hundred other leading citizens," concurring with the petitioners in the importance of convening the Legislature.

[John Speer said, in his Bismarck Grove speech: "Gen. Jas. H. Lane commenced a canvass of the Territory, holding meetings to urge the Governor to call the Legislature in extra session, to provide for a fair vote on the Lecompton constitution. He traversed the Territory, sometimes on horseback, sometimes on foot, addressing assemblies in villages, in schoolhouses, and under the trees." The facts were, as the reported proceedings of those meetings will show, he was laboring to induce the members to meet in *voluntary session* at "Lecompton, on the 3d day of December, to *suggest* such measures and adopt such action as the crisis demands." He had been elected Senator under the Topeka Constitution, and every movement of his, as we can furnish abundant proof, was looking toward a setting in motion of that government, hoping through the turmoil induced by it he would rise to higher prominence. The proposed action, through Gov. Stanton, was not of his origination; but he came into the support of the measure, as he did of sundry others, when his own pet schemes failed, and his partisan friends would always represent him as the father of the idea. The reader will excuse this digression in the interest of truth.]

The proclamation was published on Tuesday, in an extra of the Lecompton *Democrat,* and the Legislature, agreeably to its provisions, assembled at Lecompton on the 7th of December.

That body was formally organized, after which an act was passed submitting the Constitution to a vote of the electors on the 4th day of January, 1858, the same day and at the same places the election was to be held for officers under the Constitution, but with different judges and clerks. An act was also passed making provisions against fraudulent voting; and, in defiance of the solemn written pledge of the members of the Legislature, endorsed by Gen. Lane, a law was enacted over the Governor's veto, providing for a Military Board, with Lane at the head. This bill was engineered through by Lane and his friends, to the lasting discredit of all concerned in it.

CHAPTER XIX.

The Contest Begins.

ALL OUR advices from Washington showed conclusively that the friends of Free Kansas had nothing to hope from that quarter. The President, in his annual message, on the assembling of Congress, showed that his sympathy was with the framers of the bogus Constitution.

A Free State delegate convention, which proved the largest ever held in the Territory, was called by the joint action of G. W. Smith, Chairman of the Ter. Ex. Com., and G. W. Hutchinson, Chairman of the State Ex. Com., to be held at Lawrence on the 2d of December, "to take into consideration the present political situation of the Territory." This body was organized with Charles Robinson as President. By resolutions it declared that everything connected with the Lecompton Constitution from its inception was a swindle, and that the people would gain nothing by voting down the fraudulent provisions relating to slavery; that, taking into consideration the whole facts, it was not advisable to participate in the election of the 21st of December. This position was unanimously adopted by the press and people.

The Herald of Freedom, while it coincided fully with the action of the Convention, as far as expressed in that direction, insisted that it was our duty to engage in the election for officers under it, on the 4th of January; that we had the power to elect them;

that by getting control of the offices, even if Congress should admit us a State, we could refuse to organize under it; or if it was deemed wise to organize, we could call a new Convention and frame a new Constitution to meet our wishes, and that in disregard of the ten years' restriction prohibiting its amendment.

These positions were pressed with such force by editorials and communications, and the active workers in our Free State organization were so clamorous in this direction, the Chairman of the Territorial Executive Committee, who had been authorized to re-convene the Convention, if the public exigency demanded it, determined to do so, and issued the call for it to re-assemble at Lawrence on the 23d of December.

The body came together in the Congregational Church, in West Lawrence, at 10 o'clock on Wednesday. As many of the organized counties were without delegates, the letter-writers and their sympathizers appeared in force, and claimed seats. This was very readily granted. Then it was proposed the delegate or delegates acting for a county should be entitled to cast the full vote of such county. By this provision, the control of the convention passed into the hands of those who had opposed the voting policy from the beginning. On the afternoon of Thursday, the 24th, the yeas and nays were called, when 47 delegates voted in favor of participating in the election for officers, and 44 against doing so. This majority of names embraced the old, substantial, self-sacrificing hard workers, from the first settlement of the Territory, who had labored in season and out of season to make Kansas free. Opposed to them were the members of Gen. Lane's secret organization, his indorsers, their sympathizers, and the radical correspondents of the eastern press. Though in the minority in numbers, by the packing of the Convention, and voting by *districts*, the opponents of voting had a count of 75 nays to 64 ayes.

And this result was reached by an artful ruse of Gen. Lane and his backers, which is worthy of note in this connection. Just as the vote was being taken, *Gen. E. B. Whitman* appeared on the scene, and asked to be heard. He represented that he had left the camp of Gen. Lane, near Sugar Mound, in Southeastern Kansas, on Tuesday night, at nine o'clock; that he had ridden continually, changing horses four times, having been twenty hours in the saddle; that he had traveled one hundred miles, stopping to eat but one meal on the whole route, to bring the Convention the intelligence. He said Gen. Lane had about two hundred men under his command; that he had a strong position; was well supplied with provisions, and was expecting an attack the next day from one hundred United States troops and a large force of Missourians. He further stated that Gen. Lane had issued a proclamation stating that war had been made upon the peaceful, unoffending inhabitants, and that he had consented to take command of the people, at their urgent solicitation, to resist aggression; that all persons taken in arms from Missouri, who were arrayed against the people of Kansas, would be put to death; that he is only acting on the defensive, and when the attempt at subjugation shall be abandoned, his command will return to their ordinary avocations.

Gen. Whitman went on to say, that persons were marching forward from all parts of the Territory to the scene of excitement, to stand or fall with Gen. Lane and his brave command. He represented the danger as imminent, and the probability is that the contest will become general. After this statement he proceeded to harangue the Convention, charging them with wasting their time over a question of no importance whatever, while the real battle was being fought between freedom and slavery in Southern Kansas. "This is no time for hair-splitting questions," said he, "but it is the moment for brave and vigorous action."

The frenzied orator was doubtless familiar with Homer's Iliad, and gave in his own words Book II, lines 966 to 971:

> "Cease to consult; the time for action calls;
> War, horrid war, approaches to your walls!
> Assembled armies oft have I beheld,
> But ne'er till now such numbers charged afield.
> Thick as autumnal leaves, or driving sand,
> The moving squadrons blacken all the strand."

Whitman's wild manner and excitement were extended to the audience. Hinton, falsely representing Breckenridge county, being a resident of Lawrence, sprang upon a seat and called for three cheers for Gen. Lane. The vote was taken immediately following this episode, with the results stated.

After packing the Convention on Wednesday, it was very apparent the result desired would be attained. On that evening about thirty members of the Convention held a meeting at the Herald of Freedom office, when the situation was discussed, and the fact was shown that the Convention was controlled by a secret organization, at the head of which was Gen. Lane, Whitman being understood as second in rank. This fact was demonstrated a day or two after Whitman's crazy speech, by the redoubtable General, who was "on the eve of fighting the United States troops," appearing on the streets of Lawrence congratulating his friends on the result of the Convention. Those thirty men, before mentioned, resolved that the people were not willing to remain inactive; that all they needed was a ticket, composed of tried and true men, who could be trusted to take charge of the Lecompton Constitution and destroy it. They instructed W. Y. Roberts, who was one of their number, to announce from the platform, immediately after the result should be reached, if adverse to voting, that all who were in favor of putting a ticket in the field, and would sustain such ticket, to meet at Masonic Hall, at seven o'clock that evening, for such action. Mr. Roberts accepted the trust.

On my way to the Convention, on Thursday morning, I fell in with Thomas Ewing, Jr., of Leavenworth. He was a member of the law firm of Ewing, Sherman, and Denman—the afterwards Gen. W. T. Sherman, so well known to the whole country—and Mr. Ewing, with a Major General's commission, also distinguished himself in the war of the Rebellion, as since on the floor of Congress. He said he had a letter from his father, the Hon. Thos. Ewing, of Ohio, that his father was of the opinion we would be admitted into the Union by act of Congress, under the Lecompton Constitution; that the only instrumentality remaining in our hands to make Kansas free, was to get possession of the offices under that Constitution, then we must change the instrument through a convention called by the Legislature, and make one to meet our will. He said he was very anxious the people should engage in a contest for the offices, and it would require hard work to organize in the short time remaining until the election; but he would give the committee in charge of the duty $200 to pay for tickets and the expense of organizing for the brief campaign.

When the result of the vote was announced in the Convention, I made my way direct to Mr. Roberts, and requested him to make the announcement agreed upon the night before. He said the feeling of the people was such it would be useless to put in nomination a ticket. I labored earnestly with him, but he positively declined to act. I next called on Gen. S. C. Pomeroy, who was also with us. He expressed great sorrow for the result; thought now there was no doubt Kansas would be a slave State, and that all our efforts to the contrary would prove a failure. I asked him to make the announcement. He, too, declined. I next found P. C. Schuyler, of Burlingame, and begged him to give the notice. With tears streaming down his cheeks, and his voice half suppressed with emotion, he said: "Kansas is 'lost, lost to freedom! Nothing remains to us but to pack our goods and leave the Territory to its fate." Dr. Jas. Davis, of Leavenworth, also one of the thirty, refused, and desponded as to the future.

The convention was rapidly breaking up, and members were leaving, though an adjournment had not been declared. I was almost wild with anxiety. In this dilemma I met Mr. Ewing—Kansans, let his name be immortal! I hurriedly told him what I had done, and of the answers. Said Ewing:

"Who of these showed the most feeling in the premises?"

"Judge Schuyler."

"Where is he?"

Getting upon a seat, and looking over the heads, I saw his fine manly form, and pointed him out to Ewing.

"Come with me," was his response, and we were soon by Schuyler's side. Ewing, addressing Judge S., said:

"Come with us." Turning to me, "Who next has the most interest in this matter?"

"Gen. Pomeroy."

We soon found him, and Dr. Davis, and to all "Come with us," was Mr. Ewing's imperative command. Without a word of explanation we moved in a body, under the command of a master mind, to Gov. Roberts, whom Ewing addressed:

"Why don't you make the announcement you agreed to last night?"

"It is no use."

"This is not the time to discuss that question. You agreed, as a gentleman, last night, to make the announcement, and we now want you to do it. Say, if you prefer, that you are requested to do so. You need not assume any responsibility if you don't wish to."

Gov. Roberts stepped to the stand, called the meeting, still in confusion, to order, and made the desired statement.

Reader, your pardon; but I know you will excuse
the narration of an incident occurring at this moment, which I look back upon through the long years
since then with sadness and with pleasure, and which,
in its consequences, the human mind is incapable of
fathoming.

Gov. Chas. Robinson and myself had been estranged since the 3d of July, 1856. We had fallen
out while prisoners in camp. The letter-writers had
subsequently fanned our private differences into a
public flame. Like such feuds generally, ours was
but a trifling one to begin with, and if let alone
would have remained so. For nearly eighteen months
we had not spoken to nor recognized each other. He
presided at the Convention whose history we have
just written. A delegate from the Lawrence district,
his vote was recorded in favor of participating in the
election, and he made a short but very earnest and
impressive speech in the same direction.

With Mr. Roberts' announcement of the proposed
evening meeting, the convention was adjourned, and
Gov. Robinson came down from the stand, passing
through the aisles, and reached the vestibule, where
I met him, with an extended hand, and said with a
choking voice:

"Governor, can we forget our personal quarrels for
a time, and work together for the freedom of Kansas?"

The Governor seemed touched at a tender point.
Looking through moistened eyes, and showing much
emotion, he responded:

"I guess so."

We walked to a window, exchanged a few hurried

ideas as to the immediate future, and separated. While I concede so much to Thomas Ewing, Jr., which I shall more fully delineate in my next chapter, without Charles Robinson's hearty co-operation from that time forth, *I firmly believe Kansas would be a slave State to-day, with all those new States and Territories lying west and north of her to the Pacific, as well as those at the south which were such at the time of the Great Rebellion!*

And here the reader will allow me, in closing this chapter, to say, that the private animosities of CHARLES ROBINSON and G. W. BROWN were thus obliterated from our earnest determination to make Kansas free. It is hoped the recording angel dropped a tear upon the record of our foolish quarrel, and effaced it forever from his tablet. May the Governor's life be prolonged until a truthful history of Kansas shall be written, when his name shall receive the just reward of Fame, so richly merited.*

*Gov, CHARLES ROBINSON died at his home of Oakridge, near Lawrence, Kansas, August 17, 1894, aged 76 years, universally lamented. See a sketch of the Governor's Life by Prof. Canfield, in the Appendix.

CHAPTER XX.

"Brown's Cellar Kitchen Convention."

THOSE in favor of nominating a ticket under the pro-slavery Constitution, to be voted for on the 4th of January, 1858, assembled at Masonic Hall, over Woodward & Finley's drug store, on Thursday evening, Dec. 24th, at 7 o'clock, Dr. Davis, of Leavenworth, in the chair.

The attendance was quite large, much greater than was expected. The President called on the writer to state the object of the meeting, which he did at length, though in the reported proceedings the language was credited to the chair, for effect abroad. Near its conclusion a wild, hooting, disorderly rabble came streaming into the hall, filling every aisle and vacant place, jumping upon seats, and cheering at the hight of their voices. They were led by the press correspondents, and those who were interested in prolonging the Kansas strife. They were young adventurers; intent on forcing a conflict between the North and South, who had nothing to lose but everything to gain by hastening a bloody issue.

Wonder how the names of the leaders of this "incipient revolution" would appear in print, in the light of subsequent events, many of whom are still living? Since then they have been continually laboring to give credit for the grand results which followed, to those who absolutely did nothing to aid in the great work of RESCUING KANSAS FROM

SLAVERY, but positively obstructed the labors of others. Like Fame, in classic story, they demand adoration for their heroes, and are ever laboring to falsify those who oppose their claims.*

Arranging with a few friends near, while the rabble was the most furious, each made his way to a light,

---

*The ancient Romans used to personify nearly every idea, and worship it as a deity. They had a goddess whom they called Fama, in English Fame or Renown. She was represented as a messenger from Jupiter, with innumerable wings and many voices, carrying in her hand, as a symbol of her duties, a trumpet. Virgil, who knew all about the gods and goddesses, having written while they were young, says of her:

> "Millions of open mouths to Fame belong,
> And every mouth is furnished with a tongue."

She was always on the wing, journeying everywhere, in every land, spreading abroad the merits of those she would reward. Those she wished to immortalize she sang in their praise, which she repeated ten thousand times. Truth and Falsehood alike furnished themes for song. These she taught others to repeat, until the names of those she admired were on every tongue. When a hero was to be enshrined she knew no rest until her end was attained.

Fame has devotees in our day, who are as active in doing her work as were those of two thousand years ago. A trumpet blast is pealed; it rings out on the startled air; Echo catches the sound and bears it on. The wide globe is quite too small for her labors, so she builds another, and peoples it with those she loves. Those she has determined to laud she allows no one to defame. Envy, Hatred, Malice, Falsehood, and Revenge are each enlisted in her service, to destroy the influence of those who would whisper a word against the fullest accomplishment of her desires. Though no longer worshiped as a goddess, nor are chaplets woven for her brow, yet she still does service; has her devotees; enshrines her heroes, and demands their adoration. She has a long train of followers, each repeating, with increased fervor, her words of adulation, and each is laboring to crush those who oppose the popular acclaim.

which, at a concerted signal, was extinguished, leaving all in pitchy darkness.

Crowding hurriedly through the tumultuous mob, I reached the stairs on the outside of the building, and at the foot, looking up, it being star-light, I recognized many of our friends as they came down, to all of whom I said in a low voice: "Go at once to the Herald of Freedom building, and wait in front my arrival." When all had descended I ran to the office, less than a block away, opened a basement door, and directed those there to enter, though all was dark. Procuring lights, the windows were darkened with paper. [It was publicly reported and published, that I stood at the door with a revolver, and threatened to shoot any person who attempted to enter without leave. This, however, was not true. No one who presented himself for admission was refused.] When all were in the doors were locked, and we proceeded to business. There were sixty persons present, names which deserve immortality. A large number of others in sympathy, were not informed of the new place of assembling, and of course were not with us.

S. C. Pomeroy, P. C. Schuyler, S. N. Wood, H. D. Hall, John Hanna, A. Appleman, Judge J. D. Passmore, E. Heath, Robert Morrow, G. W. Zinn and Judge McKay were Vice Preisdents, with Wm. Austin, of the Kansas *Leader*, and D. H. Wier, as Secretaries. Thomas Ewing, Jr., P. C. Schuyler, F. S. Lowman, W. Y. Roberts, and J. K. Goodin, were appointed a committee on resolutions.

Resolutions were reported by the committee favorable to participating in the election, and of nominating a ticket. Among these was one declaring the candidates would be considered "pledged," should the constitution be approved by Congress, to adopt and execute immediate measures for enabling the people through another convention, to obtain such a constitution as the majority shall approve. And another, "That should Congress admit Kansas a State under that unsubmitted constitution, it will commit a gross infraction of the organic law of the Territory, and of the rights of the people."

It was at first proposed to nominate Hon. Fred. P. Stanton for Governor, but he thought, with others, that it was not wise to do so, as it was presumed there were many good men who were yet ignorant of his earnest hostility to the constitution, and that his position would be falsified by the radical press. The ticket was finally made up of the most sterling Free State men in the Territory, to-wit: For Governor, G. W. Smith; Lieut Gov. W. Y. Roberts; Sec'y of State, P. C. Schuyler; Treasurer, A. J. Mead; Auditor, Joel K. Goodin; Representative to Congress, Marcus J. Parrott.

A Territorial Committee, with S. N. Wood as chairman was appointed. At 2 o'clock on the morning of Christmas Day, "Brown's Cellar Kitchen Convention," as it was stigmatized by the radicals, adjourned for work.

I had instructed my foreman in the newspaper department to have full cases of type distributed, and every printer at his post for prolonged service.

With the adjournment of the Convention, accompanied by Mr. Thomas Ewing, Jr., I ascended to the third story of the office, not stopping at the sanctum on the 2d floor. Taking a place at the imposing stone, with pencils sharpened in quantity from thence on by Mr. Ewing, and strips of paper at hand, commenced writing up the proceedings of the last two eventful days, and such other matter as would bear upon the forthcoming election. Without leaving my place for *any purpose*, I continued to write, and the printers to put in type the matter thus prepared, proofs being taken as galleys were filled, which were read by Mr. Ewing, corrected, and immediately put into form. And thus we labored until 4 o'clock p. m., when *sixteen newspaper columns* were prepared and in type. At 5 o'clock the forms were on the power press, which was running at its highest speed.*

---

*"The Herald of Freedom helped in days of peril, especially when its editorial page was controlled by the scholarly wisdom and comprehensive insight of Augustus Wattles." So said a self-styled "Colonel," before the Kansas State Editorial Association, at Fort Scott, Jan. 23, 1900, and which the Kansas Historical Society has deemed so valuable as to copy into its Historical Collections, Vol. 6, p. 371.

It may be proper to here state, that Mr. Wattles was less than five months in the service of the Herald of Freedom. The greater part of that time was spent in collecting the material and writing the History of Kansas, which appeared on the first page of the paper, running through the entire period Mr. W. served us. He never *"controlled"* the editorial columns of the paper for a single issue. and never directed its policy.

A dozen other persons, more or less, are named by the same veracious gentleman as contributors to the editorial columns of the paper, among whom were himself, P. B. Plumb, Thomas A. Osborn, S. S. Prouty, etc., not one of whom ever wrote a line for the paper so far as I have knowledge. If they did so it was during my temporary absence for a few days from the office in selecting the town site of Emporia. They were typos and little else.

Mr. Ewing secured horses at the livery stables, with trusty riders, and dispatched them to all parts of the Territory, each setting out on his particularly designated route as soon as 500 papers could be printed and put up for him, the most distant points being first supplied. With each paper there were printed on the margin ten tickets.

We thus worked off fourteen bundles—twenty-eight reams—of paper, and forwarded them by messengers. Gen. Ewing subsequently told me he paid from his own pocket, in cash, for horses and riders on that occasion, ELEVEN HUNDRED DOLLARS, not one cent of which was ever refunded to him.

My own individual expenses I never cared to foot up, but they were very large. Much of the matter was used in the regular edition of my Saturday's paper, so all was not lost; besides a small sum was subscribed to meet this expense, but, like such subscriptions generally, only a small part was paid.

But seven days, excluding Sunday, and the reader well knows that politicians never labor on that sacred day, remained to us until the election, and we had a powerful secret organization in our own party to combat, who exhausted every resource they possessed, to keep men from voting.

Gov. Robinson wrote letters to Leavenworth, and all points he could readily reach by mail or private hands, begging all to work incessantly till the last hour, and get every Free State man to the polls, to vote down the constitution with one hand, and officers under it with the other. He visited Topeka in person, called a public meeting, and addressed it in the same direction. Night and day until after the election found him constantly at work.

Gen. Ewing, as soon as he had dispatched the papers, and made arrangements for the payment of all the messenger bills, returned to Leavenworth and organized the opposition to the constitution there, while Gen. Pomeroy did the same at Atchison, and Judge Schuyler at Burlingame. At the same time each member of the Executive Committee, of which there were seventeen, scattered all over the Territory, under the general direction of its chairman, S. N. Wood, was active.

The Lawrence *Republican*, under the editorial management of T. D. Thacher, headed the opposition to voting. "Brown's Convention" was ridiculed and treated as an insignificant affair; "indorsed by a few *sore heads* who wanted offices, political Judases, who had sold out the party, or were angered because they could not rule." Those of our Kansas readers who wish to see a specimen of newspaper bitterness, have only to consult files of the Republican, and two or three similar papers, where they will find it *ad nauseum*.

The Free State voters in most of the counties put in nomination candidates for the Legislature. So strong was the current in favor of the "voting policy" again, at a delegate convention of Douglas county, held at Masonic Hall on the 31st of December, to nominate candidates for the Legislature, under that infamous constitution, Gen. Jas. H. Lane, who was one of the delegates, and who had opposed with so much earnestness the taking of any part in the coming election, and who resorted to such a disreputable ruse to carry the late one, in opposition to voting, absolutely presided at this county convention. [See Herald of Freedom, p. 2, 2d col., of date Jan 2, 1858.]

We have neglected to state that, as contemplated by Secretary Stanton, he was removed by the President, notice of which, however, did not reach him until after the adjournment of the extra session of the Legislature. The reason given for such removal was for his convening that body. Gen. J. W. Denver, of California, who was on his way to Kansas from Washington, on some executive business pertaining to Indian affairs, was his successor, arriving at Lecompton on the 17th of December. He entered at once on the discharge of his duties as Secretary and Acting Governor. In the latter capacity, a few days after his arrival, he issued a proclamation calling attention to the recent acts of the Legislature submitting the constitution to a vote of the people, and another in regard to fraudulent voting, with an expression of a determination to bring every offender against the latter statute to speedy justice. Though understood to be pro-slavery in his views, yet he openly expressed himself in full sympathy with the positions of both Gov. Walker and the late Secretary. Like preceding Governors, he was soon on amicable terms with the conservative wing of the Free State party. Secretary Denver was commissioned Governor in May, 1858, and remained in the Territory till November 7th, when he resigned and returned to Washington, carrying with him the good wishes of the whole population.

CHAPTER XXI.

Condensed History.

IT IS not my purpose to follow future events relating to the Lecompton Constitution in detail, as histories of these are already before the public, and are accessible to all.

At the election on the 21st of December, there were returned 6,143 votes as cast "For the constitution with Slavery," and 569 "For the Constitution without Slavery." A very large majority of these votes were fraudulent. Indeed, it is questionable if they had to exceed 1,000 honest votes in the Territory.

At the election under the Territorial law, on the 4th of January, in which the Free State men participated, there were returned and counted by Acting Governor Denver, assisted by Messrs. Babcock and Deitzler, President of the Council and Speaker of the House, "Against the Constitution," 10,226; "For the Constitution with Slavery," 138; "For the Constitution without Slavery," 23.

At the election for officers under provision of the constitution, held on the same day and place with the election of the 4th of January, but with different judges and ballot-boxes, notwithstanding over 3,000 fraudulent votes were returned, 1,266 of which were from the populous city of Oxford; 729 from Shawnee, another unimportant place in Johnson county; and

1,017 fromKickapoo, all of which were counted by
Calhoun, yet the entire Free State ticket, nominated
at "Brown's Cellar Kitchen Convention," was tri-
umphantly elected by majorities *over and above all
these frauds*, ranging from 301 to 696. The Free
State party also elected 29 members of the House, to
the pro-slavery 15; and 13 members of the Senate, to
pro-slavery 6.

With this state of affairs the people of Kansas now
felt secure against the final effects of any policy that
thereafter might be adopted, either in Congress or
out of it, touching their future.

I would love to give a chapter to the "Candle-box
Fraud," wherein the election returns were deposited
by Maclean and his coadjutors, then buried out of
doors under a wood-pile, to keep them from the reach
of the Territorial Legislative Committee, and of their
being unearthed and given to the committee by the
intrepid Col. Samuel Walker, as well as of various
other criminal devices of the pro-slavery leaders to
further defeat the popular will; but I fear the reader
is wearying with our prolonged history. The facts,
however, are in reach of the general public, through
the reports of the committee, appointed specially to
inquire into these frauds, which they did in a masterly way,—Thomas Ewing, Jr., being chairman and
the most active member of that committee.*

*Since these pages were originally written Gen. Ewing pub-
lished in the Cosmopolitan Magazine, and subsequently in a
pamphlet, a full account of the unearthing of that Candle-Box
Fraud, with a general account of the Convention which paved the
way to it. Being so very important we feel justified in transfer-
ring much of it to these pages. It will be found in the Appendix, with a sketch of his life.

On the 2d of February, 1858, President Buchanan sent a special message to Congress, with the Lecompton Constitution, and recommended the admission of Kansas into ,the Union as a State under that instrument. Mr. Douglas, in the Senate, made a masterly exposure of the frauds which had characterized its history from the beginning, and led the opposition to it until its final defeat.

Gov. Walker was equally faithful in organizing and shaping resistance at Washington, and elsewhere, to secure its overthrow. Secretary Stanton, immediately after the returns of the 4th of January election were received at Lecompton, procured certified copies and proceeded with them to Washington where he joined Gov. Walker, and made an earnest personal appeal to members of Congress, with whom he had formerly associated as a member of that body, to defeat the fraud.

In April the opposition had become so strong, Mr. English, of Indiana, introduced into the House, what he called a "compromise bill," for the admission of the State. It contained many obnoxious provisions, and afterwards became a law, but as it submitted the question to a vote of the people under just and proper restrictions, which ensured fairness, no anxiety was felt for the result.

The election was held under the English bill, as it was popularly called, on the 2d of August, 1858, which resulted in a vote of 1,788 for the proposition, to 11,300 against it. A proclamation was issued by the proper officers, declaring it *rejected*, and thus ended forever the Lecompton Constitution, and its power to enslave a free people.

From the day the Free State officers were elected under that constitution its former friends lost hope in it. Aside from additional efforts at fraud, they almost wholly abandoned further attempts to fasten it on the people. Indeed, they had little motive for making other attempts in that direction, for it was clearly apparent with Free State officers to administer it,—it could no longer be used as an instrumentality to advance the interests of slavery.

Hon. C. B. Lines, at Bismarck Grove, September, '79, used this language in regard to this movement which placed that Constitution in Free State hands:

"A few of our excellent Free State men, led by Geo. W. Brown into the basement of his office, deemed it best to get up a ticket, and elect it if possible; and they did so; but the vote was by no means a general one. Not a ballot was opened in Waubansee county, and the same was true of many others. But the ticket was elected *and no harm grew out of it,* as the State was not admitted."

We regret that Mr. Lines had not stated the fact, that *that was just why it was not admitted.* And while he was seemingly pleased that Waubansee did not contribute anything in this direction, he might have told with equal truth that James Montgomery, of his way of thinking, at Mound City, after 92 votes for the Free State nominees were polled, forcibly wrested the ballot-box from the possession of the judges, and destroyed it, preventing further balloting, and causing the entire loss of the large poll already made at that point; that at Clinton forcible means were employed by non-voters to prevent the opening of polls there; and so wherever those misguided men of that faction were in the majority they attempted to defeat the people and prevent their getting possession of that constitution to either destroy it, or use it in case of compulsion, for freedom.

And thus the last of the whole series of propositions of the Herald of Freedom, of July 4, 1857, was adopted by the people, and KANSAS WAS FREE! free from the galling chains of usurpation, which had so long held the public in thrall! free from the power of a corrupt administration at Washington to longer tyrannize over it! free from the curse of slavery, and free to regulate its own institutions in its own way.

Even the Topeka Constitution was also virtually dead, and an era of peace, prosperity and happiness dawned upon the Territory.

The agitation produced by the settlement of the slavery question in Kansas, convulsed the whole country. It destroyed old parties and built a new one; it culminated in the War of the Rebellion, and ended in giving freedom to a long-enslaved race, and in establishing the principles of a republican government on a perpetually enduring basis.

Looking back upon the Past, and forward to the Future, is there a patriot who shall intimate that the anxieties and sacrifices, the toils and sufferings of the Kansas pioneers were not worthy the best days of the Republic?

And in awarding credit to those who were instrumental in producing this result, I would include the name of every person who located in Kansas, and cast his vote or used his influence for freedom; and I would also add all those in every clime, who by cheerful words, pecuniary contributions, or kindly influences encouraged or assisted the pioneer to remain there and combat the organized elements of wrong. All their names are worthy to be inscribed on a lengthened scroll, and deposited in the archives of her Historical Society, for endless preservation. And above all the rest should be written in letters of burnished gold the name of Hon. ELI THAYER, of Massachusetts, who anticipated all our movements Kansasward, organized the first Free State emigration, and continued to send it forward as our lines were decimated by desertion, disease or death; who, at his own expense, traveled more than 60,000 miles; made more than 1,000 speeches, devoted three entire years to the work without pecuniary compensation; and sacrificed a then present and prospective fortune to aid the movement; for whose head a heavy reward was offered by the secret pro-slavery lodges of Missouri; and who everywhere, on every occasion, inspired hope and confidence when that of others failed. If all other names are forgotten, his, with those of Gov. CHARLES ROBINSON and Gen. THOMAS EWING should remain imperishable.*

*While this book was being revised for publication, a letter was received from a member of the Kansas press, inquiring: "What service did the older John Brown render the Free State cause? Was he an aid or an injury to free Kansas?"

I will answer my interrogator by stating an occurrence of more than forty years ago:

Business called me in January of 1860, to my old home in Conneautville, Pa., where I founded the COURIER, published it some seven years, and where I raised a colony of two hundred and eighty persons who went out with me to Kansas. A committee representing the leading citizens waited on me, and asked me to give a public address on Kansas affairs. This was on Monday. I accepted, conditioned the meeting could be held not later than Thursday evening. This was agreed to.

I was sitting at the table of a friend to supper at 6 o'clock on that Thursday evening, when a committee called, said the large public hall was already filled to overflowing; that they had been sent to invite me not to delay the speaking to the usual hour, but to commence at once. I dismissed my supper uneaten, and made my way to Boynton's Hall. On arrival, the point of commencing the address at once burst on me with terrible force; it was difficult to crowd my way through the dense, impact body to the rostrum. Called for, I began immediately the story of Kansas' wrongs and her triumphs, substantially as given in these pages.

About 9 o'clock I noticed the hour, and seeing it was late I apologized for the time consumed, but the call from every quarter was "Go on, go on!" I did so until 10 o'clock, when I rested. A book merchant from Meadville, a Mr. Balsh, if I remember his name correctly, arose in his place, told how he had been interested and instructed, proposed all should rise to their feet, sing "Old Hundred," and that Mr. Brown be invited to continue his narration. Omitting the singing I continued with a hasty consideration of our hopes of a speedy admission as a free State into the federal Union. The audience applauded to the echo; thanked me for the address, and a rush was made to take me by the hand. At this stage some one called the meeting to order and John Brown, Jr., appeared on the rostrum. He had come there at the instance of a rival politician of mine of a few years before. He began by saying:

"George W. Brown has addressed you for more than four hours on Kansas affairs, and has not said one word about my father. He who did so much to make Kansas free, receives no attention from G. W. Brown. I deem it a gross insult to the memory of my father, and were I to meet him on the prairies of Kansas I would shoot him down as I would a dog." Hisses long continued, and John, rattling chains with which he said he was bound when marching forty miles in a boiling sun after his arrest in Kansas by the military, but which chains he never wore, was shut off.

I was again called for, and responded by simply saying: "Capt. John Brown, Sr., contributed in no way to make Kansas free. He never co-operated with the Free State leaders; he attended none of our Conventions; he did not favor us with his counsels. He never voted at any of our elections; never had a home of his own with us; his family were residents of my natal county of Essex, New York; he did not contemplate a removal of his family to Kansas, hence he was in fact and in law as much a foreigner to us as were the Border Ruffians who came from Missouri, did our voting, and made laws for us. His policy was one of blood; which the best minds labored to counteract."

And so, in my present story of the "Rescue of Kansas from Slavery" I don't know Old John Brown. He acted the part of a freebooter through all the summer of 1856, and as such he will be treated when a truthful and impartial history of Kansas is written. But it is said his murderous policy of taking five men from their beds at night and killing them in cold blood, frightened the pro-slavery party, and prevented their location in Kansas, and that so far his insane acts were beneficial.

It may be the scare-crows set up in the field to frighten destructive birds, are entitled to more credit than is the husbandman who mellows the ground, plants the seed, keeps down the weeds, and gathers the harvest; but the honest farmer views them as old clothes stuffed with straw, stick in hand, in the similitude of a man, and nothing more; so the midnight assassin who robbed and pillaged at will, accountable to no one; and he who planned and would have executed wholesale murder if not thwarted in his purpose, instead of being honored with statues and towering shafts, covered with lying inscriptions, should be classed with the scourges of mankind and consigned to an inglorious oblivion.

CHAPTER XXII.

Conclusion.*

A GENERATION has passed away since the incidents I have written transpired. Most of the actors in those times have closed their earthly record.

Kansas has become a great and powerful State, with a population of one million. Her broad and lonely prairies are now teeming with life, and beauty, and prosperity. Her long Santa Fe trains, drawn by mules, laden with merchandise, slowly winding their way to an interior Territory, have given place to two lines of railway, which daily sweep the whole length of the State, which in turn are connected by metallic bands with the Atlantic and the Pacific, while others cross these from North to South, uniting the Mexican Gulf with the Upper Mississippi and Missouri, while still others intersect these, forming a net work of iron

*The reader will remember this chapter, like the preceding ones, was written twenty-two years ago, and is here given without change; though the subsequent growth and prosperity of the State has surpassed that of any other country in the world. The marvels of romance are here excelled. An active and cultured imagination could scarcely have pictured such a glorious future as the reality presents. And the end of the greatness and glory of Kansas is not yet! When a general system of irrigation and forestry shall be adopted in practice, her barren prairies of the West will rival Egypt in productiveness and dense population, as do her people now in intelligence, moral worth and practical virtues.

rails within her borders, more than 3,000 miles in length. Wonderful change! Mighty transformation! Surely the work of the enchanter is here with his magic wand! He has touched all the wheels of active life, and they have sprung into being obedient to his will.

In the early part of November, 1854, we unloaded our press, type and fixtures on the open prairie, where now is Lawrence; then a city of tents, with a few cabins built of cottonwood; thatched with wild grass. A city of 10,000 inhabitants, with schools, churches, printing presses, manufactories, and all the appliances of an advanced civilization are there. On the high elevation, known as Mt. Oread, over which swept those heavy, searching winds when we first ascended it, on that cold autumnal morning, to get a larger view of the country in which so many important events were to be enacted, now stands the State University, the proudest institution of learning in the whole West, sending forth its educating and refining influence to all the land.

Topeka! Its site was visited by us a few months later. Beautiful in situation, a lovely landscape, a few hopeful settlers; but the rudest of cabins marked the places where now stand palatial residences and costly structures, in magnificence rivaling those of many Eastern cities. The Capitol Building, now in process of construction, at no distant day will be worthy of imitation by many older States. The city boasts a population of 15,000, and is already assuming metropolitan airs.

Emporia! Three weary days Gen. Deitzler and the writer rode over a barren prairie on horseback, to

select a town site on the "Upper Neosho." Three
more days were consumed in attempting to ford the
river at various points, to reach the location of our
proposed town. At length we found it. The earth
was covered with snow. Desolation was everywhere.
Before leaving Lawrence we had plotted it—a city on
paper—and given it a name, a new one in the post-
office directory, borrowed from a country known in
the classical era in North Africa. We were hunting
a point which in the future would fit the name—a
great commercial center. Twenty.four years have
flitted by; but Emporia, the child of the writer's
hope and brain, is there with its thriving population,
one of the prettiest towns we know, with its State
Normal School, its banks, its places of industry, its
thriving people, and its Holly system of Water
Works, and withal its brilliant future, though claiming a population of full 5,000. It has now several
connecting links of railway, where we found but con-
verging Indian trails.

Every town in Kansas, save Leavenworth and Lawrence, has been located and received its name, its
population, and its wealth since we first set foot on
her virgin soil, and looked out upon her beautifully
undulating and varied landscape.

Her prosperity, her greatness, her power, her
brilliant destiny, owe their origin to the anxiety, the
industry, the sacrifices, the good judgment and un-
swerving adherence to principle of her early pioneers.
She little recks in her present condition the ceaseless
struggles of those who laid and maintained the foundation of her future opulence.

The reader who has journeyed with us through these pages, has learned much that has heretofore been told in a desultory way. Many, even prominent actors in the strife, who shall read these Reminiscences, will be allowed for the first time to step behind the scenes, witness events and their causes never before chronicled. It has been my purpose to tell the truth, without the most distant hope of reward. If there is the slightest exaggeration of fact, or misrepresentation in any degree, the author is not conscious of it. Should such be discerned by any one, he will place the writer and the general public, as well as the future historian, under lasting obligations by calling the author's attention to it, to the end that it shall be corrected in his amended copy, which will be placed for preservation in the archives of the Historical Society of Kansas, in case it is not called for by the public to be reproduced in a still more enduring form.

The resistless stream of Time bears on its surging flood the wasting Years. Soon the last actor in these memorable scenes will sink beneath its turbid waves, and others will occupy his place. As we now look back with pride and satisfaction to the pioneers of the Mayflower, bringing to America their puritanical habits and desire for religious liberty, so may the inheritors of the free institutions planted in Kansas by our worthy compeers, look back with some kindred gratification to those who witnessed her sufferings in her natal morn, and who sacrificed much that she might be FREE !

Reader, FAREWELL !

APPENDIX,

WITH

INDORSEMENTS,

AND OTHER MATTER.

END OF THE CONTEST.

BY GEN. THOMAS EWING, JR.

*T*HE STORY of the Rescue of Kansas from Slavery would be very incomplete without the last act in the drama, as told by Gen. Thomas Ewing, a star actor, in the Cosmopolitan Magazine, of May, 1894. A few brief, and not very important passages are here omitted, to accommodate the narrative to our space. No other could have supplied the information he imparts, and much false history has been written for want of that knowledge, which has not been easily accessible. The article was entitled, " The Struggle for Freedom in Kansas." We quote :

"In February, 1854, I sat in the gallery of the Senate chamber at Washington, and heard much of the debate on the bill to repeal the Missouri Compromise of 1820. I was then about completing my collegiate course in Brown University, at Providence, Rhode Island. Four years before, I had sat in the gallery of the old Senate chamber, now the Supreme Court room, in company with Captain William Tecumseh Sherman, then in Washington from the Pacific coast, and about to be married to my sister, and heard that ever memorable debate which ended in the compromises of 1850, growing out of our vast accessions of territory from Mexico, and in the enactment of the cruel and barbarous fugitive slave law. I was intensely anti-slavery,—far more so than my Whig training would account for. I was hot with indignation at the Whig leaders who supported the repeal of the Missouri Compromise, or acquiesced in it, or resisted it but feebly. I recollect my pang of disappointment at the labored speech against the bill of Edward Everett, who was regarded as representing the conservative Whigs. It was so cool, didactic, elegant, without a glow of the indignant spirit of the North which blazed in the hearts of the people.

"The gage thrown down by the South to fight for the possession of the Territories was promptly taken up; and Kansas became the battle-ground. While studying law at Cincinnati, I watched every step in the struggle,—saw how the genius and energy of Eli Thayer taught the North to win Kansas for freedom by organized emigration, against the sporadic hordes from the populous borders of Missouri who poured over the line to plant slavery there. When admitted to the bar in the winter of 1856-7, I was married, and removed with my wife to Leavenworth."

Passing over near two pages of general Kansas history leading up to the final act under the Lecompton Constitution swindle, Gen. Ewing came to that question, and said in substance: The final crisis in the struggle for freedom in Kansas, growing out of the Lecompton Constitution, came soon after the fall election of 1857, when the Free State party, by participating in the election, had gained control of the Territorial Legislature. Then, quoting the General verbatim :

"If the Free State men should elect a majority of the State and local officers and of the Legislature, under the Lecompton Constitution, we would thereby kill that attempted usurpation in Congress, because the South could gain nothing by admitting the State into the Union, with the certainty that the Constitution would be immediately amended, prohibiting slavery utterly and forever. While, if the Free State men should refuse to vote, the pro-slavery men would control all departments of the proposed State government, and the State would, in all probability, be admitted under the Lecompton Constitution.

"The expediency of our electing officers under the Lecompton Constitution was obvious to a large majority of the Free State men of Kansas, and was well supported by the Herald of Freedom, the Leavenworth Times, and other influential newspapers of our party. That policy was also urged on us by many influential friends of free State in and out of Congress—by my father, the Hon. Thomas Ewing, of Ohio, who wrote my elder brother, Hugh Ewing, then in partnership with me in the practice of law at Leavenworth, most strongly insisting that the Free State men in Kansas, who were known to have a large majority in the Territory, should elect the State officers and members of the legislature under the Lecompton Constitution, and thus take possession of the government, and control it, so as to make Kansas a free State—just as in the then recent October election the Free State men chose the Legislature and took possession of the Territorial government. The Hon. Salmon P. Chase, then Governor of Ohio, wrote an urgent letter to Governor Robinson, advising the voting policy, which, as well as the letter from my father, was read to the Convention with great effect. The Hon. Samuel F. Vinton, an eminent member of the House of Representatives from Ohio, wrote a similar letter to me, which I read to the Convention, in which he said: 'If the Free State men shall stubbornly and fanatically refuse to adopt this policy, I for one will abandon the struggle in Congress in your behalf.'

"But that was the path leading to a peaceful solution of the Kansas strife, and many of the most active Free State leaders in Kansas did not want to tread it. They hoped for armed collisions between the Free State men and the general government, expecting that all the States would become involved, and that though the North would be in rebellion, and the South would have the prestige and power of the legitimate government, the superior numbers and resources of the North would certainly triumph. John Brown, of Osawatomie, was the inspirer, though not the active leader, of the radical wing of the Free State party. He regarded slavery as a crime, to be expiated in blood, and himself as a chosen instrument of its expiation—'the sword of the Lord, and of Gideon.' His oft-repeated maxim was, 'Without blood there can be no remission.' His dream was of the abolition of slavery by Northern bayonets, aided by the torch of the slave. He never doubted that the blacks would rise en masse, so soon as the North should be in the field to support them. He and his influential followers, mostly correspondents of Eastern papers, were, therefore, determined to defeat the proposition to vote for officers under the Lecompton Constitution, and were active and enthusiastic in securing control of the Convention, held on the twenty-third day of December, 1857.

"Charles Robinson, who had been chosen Governor under the Topeka Constitution,—a man of great ability, earnestness and honesty of purpose,—presided at this Convention and strongly urged the adoption of the voting policy. Most of the recognized leaders of the Free State party supported it—George W. Brown (now of Rockford, Illinois); S. N. Wood, P. C. Schuyler, M. F. Conway, J. P. Root, Robert Morrow, James Davis, S. C. Pomeroy, myself, and others spoke for that policy. General James H. Lane, who was by many regarded as pre-eminently the leader of the Free State party, was absent—non-committal—crafty-sick.

*   *   *

"The debate in the Convention, on the proposition to take part in the election, was protracted throughout the first day, and was very acrimonious and exciting. On the second day, December 24th, the debate went on, and the friends of the voting policy had almost silenced opposition, when 'General' E. B. Whitman, one of General Lane's political lieutenants, rode up to the church where the Convention was being held, and, dismounting from 'his steed of foam,' strode into the Convention and on to the platform booted and spurred, 'stained with the variation of each soil' 'twixt Sugar Mound and Lawrence, and in a passionate speech declared that he had just ridden eighty miles, from Sugar Mound, without stopping for food or sleep, to call the people of Kansas to arms: that General Lane was in command there, and a desperate battle was impending with the Federal troops. The excitement that followed this announcement was furious and indescribable. I sprang on a table and bitterly denounced the statement as an obvious trick and fraud to control the Convention. But the vote was forced at once, and the voting policy was rejected.

*   *   *

"While the assemblage was breaking up, I called several friends, to accompany me, and hastening to W. Y. Roberts, Vice President of the Convention, and a strong supporter of the voting policy, we persuaded him to announce to the dispersing crowd that the friends of that policy who were willing to bolt the action of the Convention would meet at Masonic Hall on Massachusetts street, at seven o'clock that evening, to nominate a State ticket and organize the Territory for the election. The announcement was received with violent denunciations and yells of dissent. The bolters' meeting, when convened that evening, was broken up by a mob, who put out the lights and forcibly ejected all the bolting delegates from the hall.* We re-convened, on the invitation of George W. Brown, in the basement of his Herald of Freedom printing-office. Only thirteen bolting delegates appeared out or sixty-four, who in the Convention supported the voting policy to the last. A Free State ticket was nominated, as follows: for Governor, George W. Smith; Lieutenant-Governor, W. Y. Roberts; Secretary of State, P. C. Schuyler; State Treasurer, A. J. Meade (now a resident of New York City); State Auditor, Joel K. Goodin; Representative in Congress, Marcus J. Parrott, who was then delegate in Congress from the Territory—all tried and true Free State men; all pledged, if they should be elected and the State admitted under the Lecompton Constitution, to favor an immediate call of a Convention to wipe out every vestige of that odious Constitution, and to frame and adopt a new one—a pledge which was exacted from every Free State candidate, big and little, nominated in the bolting movement.

"The next day—Christmas—a large edition of the Herald of Freedom was gotten out by George W. Brown, its editor and proprietor—to whose pen and purse, zeal and sense, the Free State cause, from beginning to end of the struggle, was greatly indebted for its triumphs. It was filled with arguments and information in favor of our movement, and with tickets for the Free State candidates. I hired every livery stable horse and rider that could be obtained in Lawrence, and had many volunteers, who carried the Herald of Freedom post-haste to every considerable settlement in the Territory. It will be considered, I hope, only a pardonable vanity in me to say that I personally expended in the movement over a thousand dollars—being all the money I had or could borrow. We had but nine days in which to organize and conduct the campaign, over a settled territory two hundred miles square, without a railroad.

"The pro-slavery men and newspapers fought us fiercely. Fully half of the Free State newspapers supported our movement, but the other half bitterly opposed and ridiculed it, calling our voters' assemblage 'Brown's Cellar Kitchen Convention,' and all of us 'disappointed, ambitious kickers' and 'soreheads.' S. N. Wood, of Council Grove, who had been appointed chairman of the

*Gen. Ewing was in error in this. The lights were extinguished by my direction as the best way to get rid of the turbulent mob.—BROWN.

Executive Committee by the Bolter's Convention, did great work in organizing and conducting the campaign. Never was there a nine days' canvass conducted over a greater area, under greater difficulties, or more vigorously. The result was watched in Washington and throughout Kansas with breathless interest, as likely to settle forever the vexed Kansas question one way or the other.

"At Leavenworth, a town of perhaps four thousand people, the largest in the Territory, the election was regular and the vote full, free and fair on both sides. At Mound City, in Linn county, Montgomery seized and destroyed the ballot-box and broke up the election when about half the votes had been cast. At Sugar Mound, also, the ballot-box was destroyed and the ballots scattered to the winds by a party of Free State men who were hostile to the voting policy; and so, also, at Clinton. In Wabaunsee county it was the boast of some of the extreme Free State men that the feeling was too intense there to suffer an election for officers under the Lecompton Constitution to be held in any precinct in that county. The night before the election I organized a company of about thirty armed Free State men under Captain Losee, and towards morning went with them to Kickapoo, a pro-slavery village numbering a few hundred people, eight miles above Leavenworth, and directly across the Missouri river from Weston, Missouri, a large town which had contracted the habit of sending its men at every election to swell the pro-slavery vote in Kickapoo. We rode into Kickapoo at daybreak, and had tied our horses and taken position near the polling place before the voting commenced, intending to see who voted and how many. Our appearance caused great excitement, and threats of violence, especially among the Missourians, who came from Weston as fast as the one ferry-boat could bring them. By ten o'clock, we were so overwhelmingly outnumbered that all of our troop had been induced to return to Leavenworth, except only the venerable John C. Vaughan, Wolff, Currier, and myself. We four gave our pistols to our retiring comrades, as more likely to provoke attack on us than to be useful in defense against such numbers. We then took position near the polling window, in a corner made by a projection of the building, where we might be crushed, but from which we could hardly be ejected, and there we stood all day. The voters, generally, made headquarters in several saloons, from which they poured out from time to time, noisy, drunk, armed with two revolvers to the voter—each man voting several times; several gangs voting as often as six times,—threatening us with death if we did not leave for Leavenworth. A friend of mine named Spivey, who was a clerk for Gen. Whitfield in the Kickapoo land office, and who was a sober and sensible man, acted as an intermediary between the mob and us, warning us most solemnly to leave for Leavenworth, or we would be murdered. I told Spivey, and had him tell the mob, that we would not leave until the polls should close, and they would not dare to fire on us, because they knew if they should kill one of us, the Free State people of Leavenworth would burn both Kickapoo and Weston to the subsoil before morning. Just before the polls closed, to mark the end, Mr. Currier and I voted—as we had a right to do, being citizens of that county. Our votes were numbered 550 and 551. Only two votes were cast after we voted, when the polls were closed, the total vote being 553. Whereupon, about dark, having submitted to a good deal of hustling and rough handling, we rode off for Leavenworth in a shower of rotten eggs and pistol shots.

"The returns of the election, as provided in the schedule of the Constitution, were sent to John Calhoun, at Lecompton, who was surveyor-general of Kansas, and president of the Convention. He made and published his official statement of the result in each county, showing the election of the entire pro-slavery State ticket, and a pro-slavery majority in both branches of the Legislature. His decision was prima facie correct, and beyond review or reversal by any Territorial authority. Calhoun forthwith left for Washington to report the result to Buchanan's administration, that it might be officially laid before Congress.

"Immediately on this announcement, and solely on my own impulse and initiative, I went to the Territorial Legislature, which had assembled at Lawrence in regular session, January 4, 1858, and was controlled by the Free State party, and there procured the passage of a law, approved January 14, 1858, creating a Board to investigate and report upon the frauds committed at the election on the adoption of the Constitution, December 21, 1857; and also at the election for officers under the Constitution, January 4, 1858, and in the returns thereof. Henry J. Adams, J. B. Abbott,

Dillon Pickering, E. L. Taylor, H. T. Green, and myself, composed the Board. L. A. McLean, who was Surveyor-General
Calhoun's chief clerk, was summoned to appear before us as a
witness, together with other pro-slavery men employed in the office
of the surveyor-general at Lecompton, where the election returns
and all the other archives relating to the Lecompton Constitution
had been filed. McLean appeared and swore that Calhoun had
taken all the returns relating to the elections under the Lecompton Constitution with him to Washington. This struck us as a
very improbable story; but McLean stuck to it with a respectful-
ness, dignity and sincerity of manner which were very impressive. No one could be found to throw a doubt on his statement.
We had the Surveyor-General's office at Lecompton searched for
the returns by our sergeant-at-arms; but not a scrap of them was
found. 'Our investigation, obviously, could amount to nothing
without these returns; so, with Calhoun in Washington, and his
subordinates swearing that he took the returns with him, we felt
utterly baffled and beaten.

"At a late hour of the second night after McLean's testimony
was given, as I was returning to my room at the Eldridge House,
I was accosted in the dark, on a lonely street, by a man whom I
did not know, who asked my name, but refused to give his own.
He handed me his revolver as an assurance of his pacific intentions,
saying that he had been watching on the street for me for several
hours. He said he had heard a report of McLean's testimony
before our board, and desired to know if it was given as stated. I
replied that it was. He said it was a lie, and he could prove it, if
it would do any good. He said, however; that he lived at Lecompton, and would in all probability be murdered if he should
be known to have informed on McLean and his associates. I sat-
fied him that if he could and would give me information exposing
the falsity of McLean's testimony, his action should not be
known, and that with that information, we could drive Calhoun
and his gang from the Territory, and defeat the Lecompton Constitution.

"He then said that late in the night preceding the day when
McLean appeared as a witness before our Board, he [McLean]
had buried a large candle-box under a woodpile adjoining his
office, and that he had been seen by Charley Torrey, the janitor,

who slept in the building and who told my informant. He then gave me his name as Henry W. Petrikin, and described himself as being a clerk in the office of William Brindle, receiver of the United States land office at Lecompton. This was a voucher for his good faith, for I knew enough of General Brindle to know that he would have no rascals about him.

"Next day, aided by my official position as one of the commissioners to investigate the election frauds, I obtained from Josiah Miller, Probate Judge of Douglas county, now deceased, a search warrant directed to Captain Samuel Walker, sheriff of Douglas county—who had already done loyal service to the Free State cause and was eager to do more—commanding him to enter upon and search the premises of the Surveyor-General, in Lecompton, and—if practicable—to find, take and bring before Judge Miller all the original returns of elections on or under the Lecompton Constitution. Enjoining Judge Miller to secrecy, I then sought Sheriff Walker and requested him to pick out a dozen fighting men well armed, to go with him as a posse, and told him I had a writ for him to execute, and would tell him at daybreak next morning where to go and what to do. Captain Walker was on hand punctually, with his trusty squad in a back alley; and after receiving the warrant and full instructions from me, he set out unobserved from Lawrence for Lecompton, eight miles away. He pounced upon the Surveyor-General's premises early in the morning, dug up a buried candle-box from under a great woodpile adjoining the office, and before noon he rode up Massachusetts street, in Lawrence, at the head of his squad, holding the candle-box on the pommel of his saddle.

"C. W. Babcock, President of the Council; G. W. Dietzler, Speaker of the House of Representatives; and J. W. Denver, acting Governor, met the Investigating Board in the office of Judge Miller. Sheriff Walker made return of his search-warrant and delivered the candle-box to Judge Miller, who opened and produced from it all the returns of the election for officers of the Lecompton Constitution, which McLean had sworn had been taken by Calhoun to Washington. The Kickapoo returns had swollen to 995, from 553, which was the actual vote—chiefly fraudulent—when the polls closed, there being 442 names added to the list of voters after the names of Currier and Ewing, and after the polls closed. Oxford, which had a legitimate vote of about one hundred, had the number increased in the returns, through obvious forgery, to 1,266; the returns from Shawnee showed about fifty real voters, to which had been added names—fictitious names, bringing the total up to 729. The fraudulent additions were as apparent on the face of the returns as would be extension in the leg's of a boys trowsers. They were all on the pro-slavery side; but proving insufficient to effect the desired result, a return from Delaware Crossing, in Leavenworth county, which had been honestly made by the two judges of election, was forged, by splicing with a sheet containing 336 additional names of pro-slavery voters in a different handwriting and in different ink—these fraudulent votes electing the whole legislative ticket of eleven members from Leavenworth county, and giving both branches of the Legislature to the pro-slavery party.

"These entire returns showed 6,875 votes cast for Free State candidates, and counting in all the returns, valid and fraudulent, a few hundred more for pro-slavery candidates. On the same day, the fourth of January, 1858, an election was held under a statute then recently passed by the Free State legislature, to take a vote on the adoption or rejection of the Lecompton Constitution, at which 10,226 votes were cast against it, and none in its favor. This last-named vote shows the whole strength of the Free State party of Kansas, while the vote of 6,872 for Free State candidates under the Lecompton Constitution, shows that 3,351 Free State men who voted against the Lecompton Constitution did not vote for officers under it. In other words, the Free State men who opposed the voting policy were thus shown to comprise only one-third of the Free State party.

"Immediately on this exposure—January 28, 1858—I swore out a warrant for the arrest of McLean, for perjury. But as soon as the candle-box had been dug up from the woodpile, he had fled with his fellow conspirators never to return to Kansas.

*   *   *

"The exposure of the frauds struck the Lecomptonites dumb. Every incident was telegraphed and published everywhere. On the day of the exposure, Henry W. Petrikin, who is now living at Montoursville, Pennsylvania, got a brief statement of the facts signed by the presiding officers of the two houses of the Legislature, and by Acting-Governor Denver, which statement he carried post-haste to Washington and laid before President Buchanan, in presence of Senator Bigler, of Pennsylvania; Senator Dickinson, of New York; Gen. Sam Houston, of Texas; Hon. Allison White, of Pennsylvania; and R. Bruce Petrikin, of Pennsylvania. I followed in a day or two with the report of our board to investigate the election frauds, accompanied by an abstract of the candle-box returns, and a memorial to Congress, all of which I caused to be printed at once and laid on the desk of each member of Congress.

"Thereupon, the bill then pending in Congress for the admission of Kansas into the Union, under the Lecompton Constitution, dropped dead. A few months afterwards the English bill was forced through Congress by the administration. It provided for the submission of the Lecompton Constitution to a free vote of the people of Kansas, and offered them five and a half millions of acres of the public lands for common schools and a university, and five per cent. of all the public lands in the Territory —being about two and a half millions of acres more—for internal improvements—all the grants being conditioned on the acceptance of that constitution by the people. The offer and the constitution were contemptuously rejected on the second of August, 1858, by a vote of 11,300 against the proposition, to 1,788 in its favor. Thereupon the Lecompton Constitution was abandoned, and Kansas was kept out of the Union for more than two years longer to do penance for its devotion to freedom.

"The waves which rolled high in Kansas during the political storm of 1855–6–7 extended throughout the Northern States and were long in subsiding. As late as the fall of 1860, the Kansas questions were uppermost for political discussion in every Northern State. On my way through Cincinnati to Lancaster, Ohio, during the political campaign in October, 1859, I was taken to make a speech at a Republican meeting in Fifth street, Market space, then being addressed by Tom Corwin and Caleb B. Smith. When I reached the stand, Corwin was speaking. He had been discussing only Kansas questions. As I ascended the steps, he turned and greeted me with some pleasant words of recognition, and then branched off on Kansas politics, appealing to me as a witness and a participant. He told with mock gravity of our many governments there; spoke of the Lecompton territorial government, the Topeka provisional government, the Lecompton State government, the Topeka State government, and the Leavenworth State government, and described them all as being in full operation, electing State, territorial, county, township, and city officers under each government, and all in full operation at the same time. He said it brought on a general election every month, and a county, city, or township election every other day. He said: 'My fellow-citizens: Kind and benignant nature always responds to the wants and habits ,of men; and I now make the prediction that the next generation in Kansas will be born with ballot-boxes in their bellies, like 'possums; so they can vote whenever they want to !'

"Thirty-six years have passed since the Free State struggle in Kansas ended. I have never, until recently, told all of this story to any but my own family. In making it public now, I wish not to seem unmindful of the heroism of the Free State men in the earlier phases of the contest, when many suffered capture, imprisonment and death in the cause; nor of the wisdom and forbearance of Governor Robinson and his associates, and the patriotic resistance to party dictation of Governors Walker, Stanton and Denver, which contributed so much to the happy solution of the controversy. I have written only of the last phase of that protracted struggle, which ended in February, 1858, in the abandonment of all attempts to force slavery on Kansas."

After a brief mention of the press correspondents, saying their hope of freedom in Kansas rested in inciting a war of the North against the South,* Gen. Ewing continues:

"In their correspondence with the Republican newspapers, they wrought up and magnified the incidents of the Kansas struggle in 1855–6–7, when it was a struggle of force and blood; but they were not friendly to the efforts by which the Lecompton Constitution was at last peacefully defeated. Hence the final and decisive movements which I have here narrated were ignored or under-estimated in the contemporary press, and have been almost overlooked in nearly all the histories of the Kansas struggle.

"The importance of that struggle cannot be overestimated. It was the prelude to the War of the Rebellion, and prepared the people to realize its magnitude and to resolve that it should be a fight to the finish. But for this long preparation, it is not improbable that the Rebellion would have ended in a compromise, leaving slavery, though crippled, a lasting cause of bad blood and strife between the sections. Had John Brown's purpose to bring on a war between the sections suceeeded, with the South in possession of all the power and prestige of the General government, and the North in rebellion. all the nations of the world would have stood by the South and the General government; while the North would have been divided, overwhelmed and conquered. But there was a higher power which foiled John Brown's mad scheme. The great sweep of events, from the Kansas-Nebraska bill to the surrender at Appomattox, was no doubt divinely directed to unify and purify our people for their glorious mission. Whoever bore an honorable part, however humble, on the Northern side in the great struggle, has reason to thank God for having made him an instrument in preserving this beneficent Republic, which is the hope and light of the world."

[*It has been denied by a late writer, who was born long after the events occurred narrated by Gen. Ewing. that there were two lines of policy urged for the rescuing of Kansas from slavery—one of peace, the other of blood; the peaceful policy, that pursued by Gov. Robinson and those who co-operated with him—the bone and sinew, as well the intellect of the Territory; the other that of the most prominent press correspondents, of which Redpath, Phillips, Raelf, Hinton, *id genus omne*, all foreigners and indorsers of Old John Brown and Gen. Lane, are types. Redpath placed himself on record, in his Roving Editor, a book of 365 pages, published prior to the Harper's Ferry Raid by John Brown, evidently designed to incite that rebellion. Turn to page 300, and read:

"I believed that a civil war between the North and South would ultimate in insurrection, and that the Kansas troubles would probably create a military conflict of the sections. Hence I left the South, and went to Kansas; *and endeavored, personally and by my pen, to precipitate a revolution.* That we failed—for I was not alone in this desire—was owing to the influence of prominent Republican statesmen, whose unfortunately conservative character of counsel—which it was impossible to openly resist—effectually baffled all our hopes; hopes which Democratic action was auspiciously promoting."]

IN MEMORY OF

GEN. THOMAS EWING.

THOMAS EWING, Jr., was born in Ohio in 1830. He was the son of Hon. Thos. Ewing, Sr., for many years United States Senator from Ohio, and Secretary of the Treasury under Wm. Henry Harrison.

Young Ewing at the age of 27 located in Leavenworth, and was the head of the law firm of Ewing, Sherman & McCook. He has told us somewhat of his history in the preceding pages from his pen. He was a member of the Leavenworth Constitutional Convention, and became favorably known to the prominent men of the Territory, who were members of that Convention.

On the admission of Kansas into the Union Mr. Ewing was elected Chief Justice of the Supreme Court. The War of the Rebellion coming on soon after, he resigned his office and organized the 11th Regiment of Kansas Infantry, of which he was made Colonel. For conspicuous ability and bravery, he advanced step by step, until he became Major General. His heroic conduct at Pilot Knob, doubtless saved Missouri to the Union in that bloody contest for national existence.

At the close of the war Gen. Ewing returned to Ohio, and served two terms in Congress. In 1879 the General was a candidate for Governor of Ohio, but was defeated. Removing to New York he established

GEN. THOMAS EWING.

the law firm of Ewing, Whitman & Ewing, and gained great prominence as a successful lawyer.

Gen. Ewing is best known to the people of Kansas and the Missouri border, by his famous Military Order No. 11, by which two tiers of counties lying east of the Kansas state line, and south of the Missouri, were depopulated, after the Quantrell raid on Lawrence, August 21, 1863. The "Bushwhackers," as these desperadoes were best known, had their headquarters in the afterwards depopulated region. They would come together at a given signal, invade Kansas, pillage, desolate and burn towns, murder the inhabitants, then return to Missouri laden with booty and scatter among the homes, where they would secrete themselves, until ready for another raid. But the depopulation of those counties ended that sort of warfare.

The Cincinnati Enquirer said of Gen. Ewing, in announcing his death, crushed by a cable car January 20, 1896:

"Gen. Ewing was an ideal gentleman; handsome in person; easy and gracious in manner; lofty in ideas, and he made a favorable impression on everybody he met, though he was wholly unaffected. He was a gallant and effective soldier, an able lawyer, a sincere statesman, and a politician who set a high example in the practice of politics."

Gen. Ewing always retained a profound interest in everything pertaining to Kansas, identified as he was in her pioneer history. He was on terms of friendly relation with many of the leading citizens, and continued correspondence with some of them down to the period of his untimely death.

TRIBUTE TO THE MEMORY OF

GOV. CHARLES ROBINSON.

IT WAS our purpose to write a brief sketch of the life of Governor Robinson, to accompany these pages. As we took up our pen for that purpose, and was consulting authorities for dates, and for other matters therewith, we chanced to fall in with tributes to his memory from Prof. JAS. H. CANFIELD, formerly Professor of History in the Kansas State University at Lawrence, now Librarian of Columbia University, in his review of the lately published Life of Gov. Robinson; as also an extract from the speech of Hon. CHARLES F. SCOTT, a member of the Board of Regents, and in their behalf, on the occasion of accepting from the State the custody of a marble bust of Gov. Robinson, to perpetuate his renown. As the task was so much better done by them than we are capable, we gladly accept what they say, in preference to words of our own, fully indorsing all they have said.

Wrote Prof. CANFIELD: "In its civic history and material development and in the character of its citizens Kansas has always been unique and attractive. Born in a whirlwind of political strife and cradled in a storm of National conflict, probably no State in the Union outside the original thirteen had more interesting beginnings or has kept a closer hold on the attention of the country at large. It has known all the extremes of vicissitude. More than any other section of the

GOV. CHARLES ROBINSON.

Union has it experienced abounding prosperity and the very depths of poverty, immigration by thousands and emigration by hordes, National favor and high esteem, to be followed all too quickly by a fall which made it a byword and a reproach among all people. It has been devoured by locusts and by politicians and partisans even more voracious and destructive; it has been seared by the hot South winds and by burning human passions; it has suffered from months of drought and from the withering of every hope of its people; yet again and again it has risen out of all this and more, and above it all, and has shown superb endurance, most intelligent purpose, imperial determination, and magnificent enthusiasm. But, rising or falling, in honor or in disgrace, powerful or weak, Kansas has never been dull; it has always held the centre of the stage—it has always been at the focus just in time to be thrown up large upon the canvas.

In many respects, perhaps in most respects, its people have been greatly under-estimated and sadly misunderstood. No more earnest, sincere, unselfish, public-spirited block of population can be found in the Union to-day. Though weak and worn and almost wrecked by the border strife which immediately preceded the civil war, even if it were not the immediate cause of that struggle, the new State sent to the front a larger proportion of its male population than did any sister State; while women and children gathered the golden harvest, often working long after moonlight had fallen upon the fields. When the war closed, with what might be called a fraternal instinct, thousands of veterans and hundreds of civilians, all excellent exponents of the strenuous life, entered their names on the roll of Kansas citizens and began the

creation of a mediterranean republic. They built
their churches and their schoolhouses first, they
pledged personal credit to the utmost for public
improvement, they were determined to master time
and space, and quickly to make the civilization of that
Western State equal to that of any other section of
the country. As some one has wittily remarked,
"They were the people who started west and had nerve
enough to push on, instead of stopping in Ohio." In
all the years which have passed they have dreamed
dreams and they have seen visions, but in either
dream or vision the central thought, the all-inspiring
purpose, has always been the betterment of the race.
Extremists, even fanatics, many of them became—
some of them still are. Often duped or misled by
designing men and by the self-seekers who everywhere
abound, undoubtedly they have been. But from the
standpoint of purpose, intention, desire, this people
has always occupied an extraordinarily high plane of
thought and life.

Charles Robinson was born in Hardwick, Mass., in
1818. Necessity early became his stern taskmaster.
From the time he entered the old academy at Hadley
he was largely self-supporting. At Amherst Academy he made and repaired the desks and seats to pay
his tuition. For three winters he taught in the public schools. He was a student in Amherst College for
a year and a half, when threatened failure of eyesight
compelled him to drop his studies and seek medical
advice. He walked forty miles to Keene, N. H., to
find proper treatment. He became a student of med-
icine under the physician who ministered to his
relief. He commenced the general practice of medi-
cine in Belchertown, Mass., in 1843, in his twenty-

fifth year, and almost immediately became an active
citizen of the town.   At an age when the active young
man of to-day who is looking toward professional life
is still a dependent, and is but half through his course,
Robinson was an influential American citizen.   In
two years his reputation and practice had so increased
that he removed to Springfield, where he associated
with himself Dr J. G. Holland, and the two opened a
private hospital.   His zeal and intensity in all his
work, both professional and civic, broke his health in
a single year.   After an unsuccessful struggle for
renewed strength, in the spring of 1849 he made the
overland trip to California, crossing the territory
which was to be his later home.

During the two years spent in California—full to
overflowing with all the adventures of that day, years
in which he was "physician, editor, restaurant keeper,
leader of a squatter rebellion, and a member of the
State Legislature"—Robinson regained his health,
and in 1851 returned to Massachusetts.   There he
remained till June of 1854, when he started for Kansas.   From the hour he crossed the Territorial
line till the day of his death in 1894, at the age of
seventy-six, he was a conspicuous figure in all Kansas
history.   For the great part of this time he was the
very central figure.   It is impossible to write this history without granting him this prominence.   To pre-
pare his biography is to touch all phases of Territorial and State life and experience.   The first accredited agent of the New England Emigrant Aid Company, the leader of the Free State men in all their
struggles, elected Governor under the Topeka Constitution in 1856, re-elected under the Wyandotte Constitution in 1859, the first Governor after the admis-

sion of the State and during all the stress and strain
of the civil war, State Senator for two terms, Superin-
tendent of the Indian School at Lawrence—known as
the Haskell Institute,—Regent of the State University, President of the State Historical Society—this
is but a partial list of his public positions and services. In and through them all he was a typical New
Englander, intellectual rather than emotional, cool,
shrewd, calculating,—in a good sense of the word,—
self-contained, fearless, and conscientious. His chief
aim was justice and equity. His temper was that of
the Anglo-Saxon, the temper of law and order and
truth. He was philanthropic without being sentimental, generous without weakness, considerate without undue concession, intelligent in all things. And
he was a typical American citizen. In his opinion the
public business of the State or of the Nation is the
private business of every citizen; political parties are
the scaffolding with which to erect a building, not the
building itself; legislation is to concern itself with
public affairs, not with private pocketbooks; self-gov-
ernment is little more than a remarkably well-planned
co-operative scheme. He was a firm believer in a natural aristocracy, the leadership of the best because
they are the best fitted to lead, because they are the
most efficient, because they can render the largest and
most valuable public service; but he was a thorough
and sincere democrat in advocating the widest pathway, the largest opportunity for all to enter this leadership and this service."

Hon. CHARLES F. SCOTT, as one of the Regents of
the University, and in its behalf, in accepting the gift
of Gov. Robinson's marble bust from the State,
said:

"The story of the life of Charles Robinson is so
familiar here, where the greater part of that life has
lived, that it needs not be rehearsed. It is a heroic,
almost a romantic story. It is the story of a man, a
man who took early a man's place in the world, and
held it staunchly and sturdily to the end. I trust I
shall not be misunderstood when I say it is the story
of a fighter, a man so constituted that he must take
one side or the other of every question upon which
men divided; and who, having chosen his ground,
must maintain it earnestly and aggressively against
every challenger. It is the story of a wise counsellor,
of one whose brain was always cool and clear, no matter what fires might be flashing from the blue eyes.
As nearly as any man I ever knew, Charles Robinson
deserved the tribute which the Laureate paid to the
Iron Duke when he said of him that he 'stood four-
square to all the winds that blew.' He came as near
standing by himself, balanced by his own judgment,
requiring no strengthening support from other men,
either as individuals or as aggregated into parties or
churches or societies of any kind. At various times
in his life he worked with various political parties,
but when the particular object of the work was accomplished he put the party aside, apparently with as
little concern as he would lay down a tool that he was
done with. In fact no fear of any kind, either moral
or physical, ever troubled him. He said what he
thought ought to be said with as small regard to consequences as he did what he thought ought to be
done. And if the words of to-day contradicted those
of yesterday, that did not concern him, for the words
of both yesterday and to-day were honest words. He
did not know what policy meant so far as the word

might be applied to his own fortunes. He knew, doubtless, as well as everybody else knew, that he sacrificed all the political honors which a grateful and admiring people would have been proud to bestow when he severed his connection with the dominant party. But the thought, if it occurred to him, never bade him a moment's pause.

"Men of the ancestry and mould and temper of Charles Robinson do not have to hold public office to be a part of the public life of their community or commonwealth. More than thirty years before his death Gov. Robinson laid down the only elective office he ever held and retired to his farm, but as a private citizen he was hardly less a factor in the affairs of the State than he had been as its chief executive. As a contributor to the newspapers and a frequent speaker at the hustings and on the platform, he contributed his share to the discussion of the questions that during all those thirty years made Kansas the most interesting spot on earth, writing and talking, not to gain some personal end, but because the convictions within him must have utterance. As late as June before his death in August, I saw him for the last time in life, and although the pallor of the fatal illness was on his face, the old time light was in his eyes, and he talked with the old time interest and positiveness about the things that were happening in the State and the world.

"For more than a year it was my great good fortune to be associated with Governor Robinson on the Board of Regents of this University, engaged in work that was very dear to the heart of both of us, and so I learned to know him intimately. And I learned to know him to be a just man, a generous man, an inflexibly honest man, and with all his apparent austerity, a charmingly genial and hospitable man, whom one could love as well as admire.

"His death came in the fullness of time, when his soul 'was fit and seasoned for its passage,' and the end was painless and peaceful. The stalwart, manly figure of him has passed over from the gaze of men, the eyes are shut and the voice is still forever. But so long as there remains on the map of the earth a spot called Kansas, and so long as there remains even the dimmest tradition that there was a long, heroic, and finally successful struggle there for freedom, and so long as there remains one stone upon another of the stately walls of this university, which was as the apple of his eye, so long will live the name and the fragrant memory of CHARLES ROBINSON.

TO THE MEMORY OF

HON. ELI THAYER.

BY FRANKLIN P. RICE, WORCESTER, MASS.

ELI THAYER was born in Mendon, Massachusetts, June 11, 1819. He was a descendant in
the seventh generation in this country from Thomas
Thayer, the emigrant, and in the sixth generation
from John Alden, who came in the Mayflower.

Eli Thayer received his early education in the district schools of Mendon and the Bellingham high
school. Later he attended the Academy at Amherst
and the Manual Labor School, now the Worcester
Academy, at Worcester. In 1835–6 he taught a
school at Douglas, and the next four years assisted
his father in a country store in Millville. In
May, 1840, he re-entered the Manual Labor School to
fit for Brown University, and was entered a student
at that institution in the fall of that year. In 1842
he taught school at Hopkinton, Rhode Island, and
while there was elected a member of the Phi Beta
Kappa Fraternity, an honor seldom conferred before
the senior year. In September of 1844 the superin-
tendent of schools in Providence, Nathan Bishop,
induced him to take charge of the boys' high school
for the remainder of the year by the offer of $600.
This school, which had proved unmanageable in the
hands of several masters, he reduced to order and
subjection; but in consequence of these undertakings
he lost a year in college. He was graduated in 1845,

HON. ELI THAYER.

the second in his class. He immediately went to Worcester to teach in the Manual Labor School, and later became principal.

In 1845 he purchased the rocky eminence known as "Goat Hill," and in 1848 began the erection of the building called the Oread, which was completed in 1852. Here he established the famous school for young women, which he conducted with great success until he entered into his Kansas and Congressional work. He was elected a member of the School Board in 1852, was an alderman in 1852-3, and he served in the State Legislature in 1853-4. During the first year he became conspicuous by the introduction of a bill to incorporate the Bank of Mutual Redemption, which was hailed with delight by bankers and moneyed men throughout the State, as it afforded a means of release from the autocratic rule of the Suffolk Bank of Boston.

But it was in 1854 that Mr. Thayer accomplished the great act of his life, which will enroll his name among the benefactors of mankind, in originating the plan which saved Kansas and the other Territories to freedom, and settled the destiny of the nation; for if the Southern leaders had secured the Territories, it would have given them the balance of power for many years to come, and there would have been no Rebellion; the North would have acquiesced, as it always had, in the decision of a Congressional majority.

It was at a meeting to protest against the repeal of the Missouri Compromise, held in the old City Hall in Worcester, on the evening of the 11th of March,

1854, that Mr. Thayer announced his celebrated "Plan of Freedom." It was simply to take possession by lawful means of the new Territories through organized emigration of Free State men, sustained by a base of supplies. This Mr. Thayer tersely defined as "Business Anti-Slavery," distinguished from sentimental and political anti-slavery, both of which had been tried for many years and failed, slavery in the meantime constantly growing stronger. Mr. Thayer clearly saw that whichever side obtained the majority of actual settlers would control the institutions of the new section in spite of all efforts to establish others among them, and to the purpose of securing this majority for freedom, he devoted all his energies and all his means until that end was accomplished.

He immediately took measures to secure the passage of an act to incorporate the Massachusetts Emigrant Aid Company, and two months before the vote to repeal the Missouri Compromise was finally passed by Congress, hired a hall in Boston and began to speak afternoons and evenings in promotion of his undertaking. The press throughout the North and West gave wide currency to the announcement of his intention, and for a time there were indications of interest in the project. But the intense excitement and strong feeling which were manifested while the repeal of the Compromise was pending, in great measure subsided after that act was accomplished, and Mr. Thayer found extreme difficulty during the next two months in persuading a sufficient number of men to join in his enterprise to form the first colony. The Native American or Know Nothing frenzy so fully absorbed the public mind that other considerations were almost entirely excluded, and the Free Soil vote dwindled to a few thousand, the Republican candidate for Governor of the State himself deserting his party and voting with the Native Americans.

Mr. Thayer traveled over a wide section, and addressed many thousand people before he was able to revive the enthusiasm which had greeted his appeal. But after the departure of the advance colony in July, 1854, there was little difficulty, and the South soon awoke to the fact that it had at last met a formidable power. The unlawful aggression of the slave power against the Free State settlers in Kansas soon aroused the North, and the conflict which followed is familiar in history. Mr. Thayer gave all his strength, his time, his money to the work of saving Kansas, until the border ruffians and the powers at Washington abandoned the fight at the end of 1856.

He then turned his attention to the colonization of western Virginia with Free State men, and founded the town of Ceredo. His "Friendly Invasion" of the Old Dominion had the countenance of Gov. Wise and other prominent men of that section, and the undertaking progressed to considerable extent, but the opening of the war suspended the work.

In the fall of 1858 Mr. Thayer was elected to Congress as the representative from the Worcester district, and at once took a leading position in the National Legislature. His speeches on Central American colonization, on the "Suicide of Slavery," and on the admission of Oregon, brought him great fame. By the former he extinguished the hopes of the Southern propagandists, who were planning a

great slave empire, to include Mexico, Central America and Cuba; and by the latter and by personal effort
he secured the admission of Oregon into the Union
against the caucus decision of his own party.   In
this act he planted himself upon broad and states-
manlike grounds in opposition to partisan dictation,
and was sustained by leading Republican organs
throughout the country, although he received some
censure at home.   In 1860, after a most exciting canvass, he failed of re-election by a narrow margin.

During the Rebellion Mr. Thayer proposed to Secretary Stanton a plan for the military colonization of
Florida as an effective method of quelling the insurrection and restoring the Union.   The plan was approved by President Lincoln, several of the military
leaders, and a majority in Congress, and was supported by great meetings held in Cooper Institute,
New York, and in Brooklyn, but other military operations intervened and the opportunity passed, much
to the regret of those interested.   In later years Mr.
Thayer advocated his colonization scheme as a remedy for polygamy in Utah.

Mr. Thayer was the author of "The Kansas Cru-
sade," a graphic account of his great work; and he
wrote much of history for the press, to show that in
the events above recorded the present and most
important epoch of our country's history had its origin.   He died at Worcester, April 19, 1899.

Gov. Robinson, in the course of a letter in September, 1887, to Joseph A. Howland, of Worcester, Mass.,
who controverted Mr. Thayer's severe reflections on
the Garrisonian, disunion Abolitionists, indirectly in-

quired of the Governor if he indorsed Mr. Thayer's utterances, to which the Governor replied:

"Does Mr. Thayer claim too much credit for his part in saving Kansas to freedom? I think not. In a letter to the Historical Society, when his marble bust was accepted, not being able to be present, I wrote that 'Kansas can never too highly honor her early friends without whose exertions freedom would have been driven from our borders. Of the long list of names that Kansas will ever delight to honor, that of Eli Thayer stands at the head. It was his brain that conceived, and his indomitable will and energy that accomplished the organization of emigration, without which Kansas and the country would have been cursed with slavery to this hour. Let us see: During the critical period Kansas Territory was all pro-slavery except Lawrence, Topeka, Manhattan, Ossawatomie and Wabaunsee; and all these towns, except perhaps the last, were settled under the auspices of the New England Emigrant Aid Society. So it is safe to say that without these settlements Kansas would have been a slave State without a struggle; and without the Aid Society these towns would have never existed. And that Society was born of the brain of Eli Thayer. Such being my conviction, I can never cease to honor his name while life shall last.' Charles Sumner said he would rather have the credit due Eli Thayer for his Kansas work than be the hero of the battle of New Orleans; and I, if ambitious for fame in future generations, would prefer the name of Thayer to that of Lincoln, or Washington even, for while these men acted well their part in official position, Thayer invented the machinery, and engineered it, that set at liberty four millions of people."

INDORSEMENTS.

LETTER FROM SECRETARY ADAMS.

KANSAS HISTORICAL SOCIETY,
TOPEKA, May 10, 1881.

DR. GEO. W. BROWN,

MY DEAR SIR:—This Society is greatly indebted to you for the interest you take in its object, manifested in many ways, not the least of which is your history of Kansas, as given in your several publications. I sent for and am carefully preserving two copies of the papers containing your "Reminiscences of Gov. Walker." But your own copy which you give us, with your annotations, will be a valued boon.

To be sure, only a few now appreciate the value of these records of history, though written down by the actors and observers; but the number of such will increase as time lapses; and they will, for all time, regard such work as that done by you as of priceless value. I trust you will not fail to give us the Newspaper history of which you write.*

Our work of collecting newspaper history is a specialty with us, believing they are the best materials of history, and our work being for the whole State, and not for any one locality, we are saving all the papers of the State. I think we are doing better work in this line than is being done elsewhere. It is our purpose,

---

*I regret to write that the promised history of the HERALD OF FREEDOM has not been written, though many falsehoods in regard to it and its positions have assumed great prominence.—BROWN.

in our next report, to give a complete chronology of
Kansas Newspapers, and that of the HERALD OF
FREEDOM we must by all means have—the true his-
tory, with the truth as to other papers.

Yours Very Truly,   F. G. ADAMS, SEC'Y.

LETTER FROM ACTING-GOV. STANTON.

WASHINGTON, D. C., April 18, 1881.

MY DEAR SIR:—Your "Reminiscences of Gov.
Walker" is before me, and has been read hastily.
Many of the transactions you describe took place
before I went to the Territory, and I had no other
means of knowing the facts than what were gathered
from the newspapers, and the reports of those who
professed to have access to reliable sources of information.

I do not doubt you have given a correct version of
Gov. Walker's doings in Kansas, and of interviews
with him; and I think you have done good service in
the cause of truth by stating the facts bluntly and
plainly.

As regards your 14th chapter I know the Governor
had some scruples about his power to go behind the
returns. I had none, for I felt the frauds were too
palpably gross and patent, to admit of any hesitation.
Neither of us had any difficulty after we had visited
the localities, and ascertained the facts.

What you say in the 15th chapter about John
Speer's statement, in September, 1879,* surprises me

*See Speer's representation, near the head of page 180, Kansas
Memorial Volume of 1879.

greatly. I do not remember that any one threatened Gov. Walker and myself at Fish's below Blue Jacket's, or at any other place on our way down. If such an occurrence had taken place, I could hardly have forgotten it. You are certainly right in denying that any such threats influenced Gov. Walker or myself.

In your account of Gov. Walker's action in bringing troops to Lawrence, you say his proclamation was "bombastic," etc. I think myself, the proceedings in that emergency placed the Governor at a very great disadvantage, inasmuch as the restless and mischievous element of the Free State party, with Lane at their head, had the tact to deny their real purpose, and refrain from any overt acts of a decisive character; and thus the Governor's military display looked a little ridiculous.

Before Gov. Walker started for Washington I begged him to convene the Legislature. I told him if he did not do so, he would find a proclamation from me before he should reach the Federal city.

On the whole your book is valuable and interesting, as showing much of the inside operation of parties and prominent actors in the affairs of Kansas at the important period of which you write.

Very Truly, Your Friend,

FRED. P. STANTON.

LETTER FROM HON. ELI THAYER.

PHILADELPHIA, Pa., April 29, 1881.

DEAR SIR:—It gives me pleasure to acknowledge, with many thanks, the receipt of 20 chapters of your

"Reminiscences of Gov. Walker," as they have been published.

It is fortunate for the history of Kansas, as well as for the history of the United States, that the decisive struggle between freedom and slavery should be recorded by the facile pen of one who can truthfully say, as did Æneas:

"All that I saw and part of which I was."

Allow me to express the hope that no obstacle may prevent the continuance of these narratives so long as the minutest details of this epoch of our country's history—most potential in results—shall remain unrecorded.

It is fortunate, also, that you have begun this great work while there are many still living who are ready to bear witness to the truthfulness of your words.

Of the minute details of political action in the Territory at the time of which you write I have learned more from your pen than I ever knew before.

From the very first agitation of the repeal of the Missouri Compromise, early in the year 1854, to the end of 1856, my thoughts and efforts were confined to one idea. That was to keep at all times in Kansas a strong majority of Free State men. Always after the end of the year 1854 we had such a majority. That was the one grand point, and I cared but little for Shawnee Legislatures, Lecompton Constitutions, or the pro-slavery tendencies or sympathies of the territorial officers. All these were only the foam on the sublime waves of Freedom sweeping over the prairies towards the setting sun. To submit to the inevitable was the sensible thing for slavery to do at that time, for to resist those waves in their majestic progress was to make one tidal wave which would bury slavery in oblivion. That was done by the Rebellion.

Hoping you may continue to revive these memories of the great struggle, "the cause of causes," I remain,

Very Truly Yours,   ELI THAYER.

GOV. ROBINSON'S INDORSEMENT.

LAWRENCE, Kan., Jan. 26, 1881.

FRIEND BROWN:—So far your "Reminiscences of Gov. Walker" are very interesting, and strictly accurate so far as they cover matters of which I was cognizant.

On the 29th of March Gov. Robinson wrote again:

I have read all your chapters with increasing interest, as they appear, and as yet find nothing to criticise. Your chapter 16 contains much that was not personally known to me, but so far as I do know it is correct. Kansas history would be very incomplete and one-sided without your statements, and I am very glad you have lived to make them. Heretofore the effort has been to make all matters hinge on a few conflicts, on a few insane movements, ignoring the vital questions that decided the contest in favor of freedom. It is high time the truth was told, and the whole truth, and your "Reminiscences" were written. No one else has the material and facts to write this part of our history as well as yourself, and I feel that we owe you more than we can ever pay for your services to the cause of truth.

After completing the work the Governor wrote again, as follows, on May 2, 1881:

I have just finished reading the slip containing the "Conclusion" of your "Reminiscences of Gov. Walker." To say that I have read every line with deep interest and great pleasure, is but half the truth. I am exceedingly pleased that the political history of Kansas is at last being recorded, and by so able and competent a pen as yours. No person can better write of these events than yourself, as you are a very important part of them, and were in a position to learn every material fact.

You and I well know that the struggle in Kansas was chiefly political, and it was the policy adopted by the people which saved the Territory to freedom, and not the incidental skirmishes in a few localities. Unyielding devotion to principle and unflinching moral and physical courage were essential, but without political sagacity all would have been lost. In every instance the policy we advocated was adopted by the people, so far as I remember, always excepting some impracticables, demagogues, and a few well meaning persons.

*   *   *

I am more and more convinced that it is your duty to keep your pen employed till it has covered the whole field of the Kansas struggle. Posterity will do you ample justice, if the present generation does not. Should you continue, and publish your writings in book form, it will be more valuable than all the works of the kind I have seen, and I have no doubt will be in great demand.

Very Truly,   C. ROBINSON.

LETTER FROM GENERAL EWING.

FIFTH AVENUE HOTEL,
NEW YORK, May 6, 1881.

DR. G. W. BROWN,

DEAR SIR:—I have read with great interest and pleasure your "Reminiscences of Gov. Walker." I took no prominent or active part in the public events therein described, except in the 23d of December Convention, and in the campaign and election which followed it; and in the signal exposure of the frauds by which the attempt to make Kansas a slave State was baffled and finally defeated. So far as your narrative covers these most important events, I believe it to be a valuable contribution to the history of the ever memorable struggle for the freedom of the Territories, and fully accurate.

Very Truly Yours,   THOMAS EWING.

LETTER FROM COL. WALKER.

LAWRENCE, KAN., MAY 9, 1881.

FRIEND BROWN:—I see by the last Gazette you have concluded your very interesting "Reminiscences of Gov. Walker." The subject of your recollections never had justice done him by former writers on Kansas affairs, and I am pleased to know there is one man living who has the courage and ability to write the true history of those dark days. It takes more courage than I possess—and I always thought I had a good share of it—to write the truth about those times, while so many of the participants still live to criticise each trifling error. I believe I could face a twelve pound battery without flinching; but I could not write of those early times and endure the bitter personal assaults from those who had less opportunities for observation than myself, which would be sure to follow.

Much of our history has been misrepresented. You had opportunities of knowing much that was transpiring which was hidden from others. I was located near the Border Ruffian capital; was forced into repeated conflicts with the conspirators, and participated in all the troubles to the end. Appointed U. S. Marshal, and elected Sheriff—the first Free State man serving in those capacities—I think I can tell when genuine Kansas history is written. Of course you saw many things which did not come under my personal observation. We used to wonder who was the correspondent of the St. Louis Republican, and talked of the correctness of the reports from Kansas during the autumn of 1857. I own 1 was greatly surprised in reading your Reminiscences, to learn that you were their author.

On Gov. Walker's first arrival in Kansas, he sent for me, and we had a long conversation. He said he had heard of my affair with Col. Titus and others; that I was a native of his own State, of the same locality and of the same name. We even found we were of the same family. He always treated me afterwards with great kindness and confidence.

You are correct in your statement that I was in the Governor's tent and heard the conversation reported by you in regard to the collection of taxes, etc., as detailed in your 11th chapter, and I can vouch for the truth of what you have there written. I was also a member of the secret organization which you mention, but I am glad to write, *I never favored the murdering policy.* I was always for open war, not secret assassination.

Govs. Geary, Walker, Stanton and Denver, all, were in favor of "equal and exact justice to all men," and, consequently, were true to the Free State party, though known as Democrats. Republican as I am, it gives me pleasure to know that you have done justice to all of them.

You may be interested in an incident in which I took a small part. While the Lecompton Constitutional Convention was in session the Governor's signature was desired for some purpose. He refused to give it. The Ruffians threatened to take his life. He fled to Secretary Stanton's cabin, on the river three miles east of Lecompton—where you and Robert Morrow found him on the 19th of October—and dispatched his then Aid, Capt. Walker, of the regular army, to me to come and help defend him. We found Mr. Stanton and the Governor, with another man, and at once barricaded the doors and windows for an attack. About ten o'clock at night we were visited by a man from Lecompton, who said the leaders had learned of the Governor's hiding place, and had determined, if he would not sign his name to the instrument, to kill him. But the Governor remained firm and unflinching, resolved to die before he would do what he conceived a wrong. At the same time some of our own party were abusing him because he was a Democrat. We remained on guard until 4 o'clock in the morning, when I was sent to Lecompton to learn what was transpiring there. I found the

HON. ROBERT MORROW.

saloons full, but soon came to the conclusion from what I heard, that their threats were *bluster*, so I returned and reported, and was soon after discharged from duty. Very Truly Yours,

SAMUEL WALKER.

LETTER FROM CHAS. S. DUNCAN.

LAWRENCE, Kan., May 8, 1881.

DOCTOR BROWN:—With regard to your "Reminiscences of Gov. Walker," I am glad to say, after a careful perusal of the work, it embodies the exact facts, in every essential particular, as they came under my personal observation. In reading I could not but feel grateful that one of the "old guard" survived who could so truthfully and minutely record every important event occurring during the period of which you write. I assure you, Friend Brown, that your work is highly prized and shall be carefully preserved.* Yours Respectfully, C. S. DUNCAN.

*See p. 107. Mr. Duncan is still living at Lawrence. He was one of our earliest and most substantial merchants.

LETTER FROM HON. ROBERT MORROW.

LAWRENCE, Kan., April 21, 1902.

DOCTOR BROWN—DEAR SIR:—I have read the advanced sheets of your forthcoming "Reminiscences of Gov. Robert J. Walker, and the True Story of the Rescue of Kansas from Slavery," with great interest. Your statements are very interesting, and so far as I have knowledge are strictly truthful.

You understood Gov. Walker better than most of us. I greatly regret our people did not treat him with more consideration, and not with so much distrust. He gave us good advice, and faithfully observed his promises.

I remember going with you to Lecompton, to invite the Governor to come to Lawrence. We found him and Secretary Stanton, two miles east of Lecompton, occupying a log cabin in the woods, near the bank of the river. You describe very accurately the incidents of that interview.

I lived at Lawrence all the time you mention, and was conversant with all the leading events as they transpired. I was a member of the Committee of Public Safety, of which you were one, as were Charles Robinson, Jas. Blood, Wm. Hutchinson, C. W. Babcock, G. W. Smith, Lyman Allen, Samuel Walker and G. P. Lowry, the latter serving as chairman; and was intimately concerned with every important event connected with the Free State cause. I was one of the party after the fall election of 1857, who went to Oxford to look after the frauds there perpetrated. On our return we met Gov. Walker and Secretary Stanton on their way there.

My recollection is, that I went with you on a second occasion to see Secretary Stanton, then serving as Acting Governor. Gov. Walker had left Kansas. Our object was to induce him to convene the Territorial Legislature to head off the Lecompton Constitution. Gov. Stanton said it would cost him his official head, but he encouraged us to expect a proclamation from him in the direction we asked.

In looking over the names mentioned in your book

as in attendance at the Grasshopper Falls convention, where the voting policy was fully adopted, I think you and I only remain. All the rest have joined the silent majority, but the people of Kansas are enjoying the rewards of their labor.

We have Gov. Walker, yourself, and those who acted with you, to thank for the glorious outcome. Even after we gained control of the Territorial Legislature there were persons so unwise as to urge that the Territorial Legislature adjourn *sine die*, and give place to the Topeka government. I was a member of that Territorial Legislature, and was well posted in the movement. Those who favored it were very indignant because the Territorial government, then in Free State hands, and was being wielded for freedom, would not give way to the new project.

I know well the element you had to contend with which did you all the injury they were capable, but you have outlived them all. You have done a valuable work in writing your history. It is only justice to the memory of Gov. Walker that you, who know the truth so well, should relate it for the benefit of posterity. Yours Truly, ROBERT MORROW.*

*Mr. MORROW came to Kansas in the early spring of 1855, and located in Lawrence. He identified himself from the beginning with the Free State party, and with the material interests of the city, and was one of our most trusty advisers on all political questions. He erected the Morrow House, the first creditable hotel in the city, which was greatly esteemed under his excellent management. Mr. Morrow was a member of the Territorial Legislature and voted for the repeal of the bogus statutes, and served one term in the State Senate. Faithful to every trust, he and his good wife, both far advanced in years, are still in Lawrence where they probably expect to spend the residue of their lives. May they be long protracted. Mr. M's photogravuer faces these pages.

THE LAST WORDS.

HE PRO-SLAVERY party which had usurped the Territorial government of Kansas, and administered it in the interests of slavery, in casting their eyes over the field, and seeing who were their most active opponents, indicted by a servile Grand Jury, under instruction of a violently partisan Court, Charles Robinson, G. W. Brown, G. W. Smith, G. W. Deitzler, and Gaius Jenkins, for constructive high treason, an offense unknown to our laws. Yet these men were arrested and held as prisoners under that false charge for four months, guarded by a regiment of United States troops. It is reasonable to suppose the enemies of free institutions knew very well from whom they had most cause to apprehend danger to the success of their vile measures. During that unjust imprisonment the prisoners received from the Poet Whittier "Lines" inscribed to them, see p. 108 of his "Panorama," published in 1856, of which the following is the closing stanza:

"God's ways seem dark, but, soon or late,
 They touch the shining hills of day;
 The evil cannot brook delay,
 The good can well afford to wait.
Give ermined knaves their hour of crime;
 Ye have the future grand and great,
 The safe appeal of Truth to Time."

Relying upon that assurance, amid all the malicious slanders, libels and distorted history, the writer has been conscious that another generation, with an enlightened vision, would discern who were the REAL heroes that RESCUED KANSAS FROM SLAVERY and award them that merit heretofore rendered to aspiring demagogues, and brutal midnight assassins. These deliverers were the honest, conscientious toilers who went to Kansas in advance of the "heroes," taking their families and their fortunes with them, and who labored in season and out of season to build up homes free from the curse of chattel slavery.

Gov. Robinson, on numerous occasions, declared it was not the politicians, nor aspiring ambition, which produced the result; but it was the product of honest votes, cast by honest men in a righteous cause, that made Kansas free. He predicted another generation would give credit to those who were entitled to it, however numerous the garbled accounts of fiction-writers who make history from reports of interested, sensational and untrustworthy press correspondents, who were more zealous for the compensation given for those services than they were for truth. This prediction of the Governor, is well expressed in the axiom:
"Time fights the battles of Truth, an unwearied and unimpassioned ally."

This truism is already being verified. There are a few writers, without reputation, who take their cue from the unreliable correspondents; but the better class of historians have investigated for themselves and do not believe, as one of those romancers asserts, that the Sovereign Ruler of the Universe inspired assassination, and projected the murder of men and boys to carry forward a great reform. Of such we are glad to mention a recent work by Prof. J. W. BURGESS, of the Kansas State University, in his Middle Period, published by the Scribners in 1897, p.471:

"With the rejection of the Lecompton Constitution by the people of Kansas, on August 2nd, 1858, the struggle for Kansas was closed. It was to be a non-slaveholding Commonwealth and a Republican Commonwealth. The record of this struggle is certainly one of the most remarkable chapters in the history of the United States. There is much to admire in it, much to be ashamed of, and much to be repudiated as foul and devilish. The prudence, moderation, tact, and bravery of Dr. Robinson and his friends have rarely been excelled by the statesmen and diplomatists of the New World or of the Old. They were placed in a most trying situation both by their foes and by those who, professing to be their friends, endangered the cause more by violent and brutal deeds than did their open enemies. Their triumph over all these difficulties is a marvel of shrewd, honest, and conservative management, which may well serve as one of the best object-lessons of our history for succeeding generations."

Other historians have expressed themselves no less emphatically. With the whole truth, long suppressed, in their possession, there will be but one voice in the premises, and that in denunciation of the offenders, of which the words of the lamented Winwood Reed are specimens:

"Murder is not less murder because it is conducive to development. *There is blood upon the hand still, and all the perfumes of Arabia will not sweeten it.*"

And Æschylus: "Not all the world poured in one libation, can atone for one man's blood."

Then Sophocles: "All the rivers of the earth cannot wash away the pollution which clings to the house and family of the murderer."

Such sentiments will be echoed the wide world over when reason and an enlightened judgment gain control over the passions and prejudices of ignorance and anarchy. FAREWELL!

May 15, 1902.

CONTENTS:

204 CONTENTS.

ILLUSTRATIONS: